Super Parents

Super Children

To Donna,
Happy parenting!

Frances Kendall

Leon Louw

Super Parents Super Children

Frances Kendall

Illustrated by the author

Foreword by Strilli Oppenheimer

American Book Distributors, Inc.
Spring Mills, Pennsylvania 16875
(814) 422-8061

ISBN 0-929205-00-6

LIBRARY OF CONGRESS CATALOG CARD NUMBER 88-71634

MANUFACTURED IN THE UNITED STATES OF AMERICA

TO MY FATHER

Your children are not your children.
They are the sons and daughters of Life's longing for itself.
They come through you but not from you,
And though they are with you yet they belong not to you.

You may give them your love but not your thoughts,
For they have their own thoughts.
You may house their bodies but not their souls,
For their souls dwell in the house of tomorrow,
which you cannot visit, not even in your dreams.
You may strive to be like them, but seek not to make them like you.
For life goes not backward nor tarries with yesterday.
You are the bows from which your children as living arrows are
sent forth.

from *The Prophet*

by Kahlil Gibran

Contents

Foreword

It has given me great pleasure to be asked to write the foreword to Frances Kendall's book, *Super Parents, Super Children*. I enjoyed the book, and I feel it could be really useful for many people who are looking for a formula for happy relationships between themselves and children.

This book contains a great deal of common sense—a commodity which seems sadly lacking in the nurture of children today. At a time when parents are constantly asking for "a method" or "complete answer" on how to bring up their children, Frances Kendall has the confidence to say that she does have that answer. In as much as she is always consistent in her respect for the child as an individual person and that her philosophy is what used to be called COMMON SENSE, I recommend this book to those confused parents and adults with responsibility for children, as an answer.

Acknowledgments

To my husband Leon, for introducing me to libertarianism, for helping me formulate my ideas, and for being a constant source of stimulation. To my mother and father, for raising me so well, despite not have this book. To Libby Husemeyer for her support and encouragement. To Eustace Davie, for our long and fruitful discussions. To all of these people, as well as Mark Swanepoel and Judith Ryder, for reading the manuscript and making helpful suggestions.

Introduction

The average relationship between parent and child is characterized by disappointment, frustration, conflict, and pain. Some parents accept this situation as unavoidable. Others turn for help to the rash of child-rearing books which have appeared in response to their needs. Unfortunately, these books are almost all confusing and contradictory. They offer good ideas for solving problems in specific situations, but they have no simple rules which can be applied to all age groups and all problems.

Here, this book departs radically from the standard literature. The methods it describes are based on a simple philosophy which is consistently applied to all aspects of the parent-child relationship. It provides basic guidelines which can be easily applied to any new problem which arises. It aims to show that parents and children can live in mutual respect, esteem, and happiness, and share the same values—values so elementary that they can be thoroughly integrated by the age of five.

Because this book advocates that parents treat their children as they would another adult, some of the ideas may at first seem radical or even outrageous; however, if they are given a fair trial, success will prove their validity.

At present, most children are taught throughout their formative years that adults always know far better than they what is good for them. They are encouraged to obey orders, rather than to make decisions. They are expected to respect adults, but receive no respect in return. Because children are small and unable to defend themselves, adults are able to coerce them by physical force.

Small wonder that when they grow up, they turn to the state or church to make their decisions for them, in the place of their parents and teachers. They have never been given the chance to develop confidence in their own abilities. The message has always been, "You are too small, weak, silly, and inexperienced to know what is right or wrong."

If children were reared by the sometimes revolutionary methods outlined in this book, the world would be peopled with assertive, independent, and confident young. They would understand that "there is no such thing as a free lunch," and that the responsibility for their happiness lies in their own hands. They would have no need or desire to impose their will on others. That would indeed be a fortunate world to bequeath to our descendants!

1

Goodbye to the Hit and Miss Method

If you would like to have the joyful experience of sharing your home with happy, confident, independent, responsible, and self-disciplined children, then this book is for you.

The following pages hold the solutions to your child rearing problems, and the key to happy family interaction.

These solutions are based on a surprisingly simple and consistent set of principles. Each chapter shows how these principles can be applied in real situations which arise in day-to-day living with children.

Many of the ideas in this book are not new. They have been discussed in detail in other books, some of which are not specifically concerned with child rearing. Now, for the first time, they have been brought together and coordinated with new concepts to form the basis of an original and significant theory of parenting.

In *The Child Under Six*, James L. Hymes, Jr. says: "The human child is a social creature. His sociality is a quality of the utmost significance...children want to live with others. They have built into them a very special super sensitivity to all those things which make living with humans possible. The whole direction of their growth—their internal maturation—is toward the ways of acting that make human society possible."

I believe that this statement is true, but most people would say the opposite. They would say that the whole direction of children's growth seems to be toward the ways of acting that make human society impossible!

Most people, when they decide to start a family, have a pretty hazy idea about why they are doing it. A couple gets married, and then maybe without any planning, the woman becomes pregnant; or perhaps after one or two years, they decide that now they would like to have children. That is what everyone else does, and it seems the natural pattern to follow. Once a baby is on the way, the mother especially, and often the father too, looks forward to the new arrival as something which will generally enrich their lives. Unfortunately this seems seldom to be the case.

In the introduction to *Kids Day in and Day Out,* the editor writes: "Until we had kids most of us believed that raising children is fulfilling and 'natural' . . . but it is hard, bewilderingly and painfully hard." Adele Faber and Elaine Mazlish of *Liberated Parent, Liberated Child* start their book: "It didn't add up, if what I was doing was right, then why was so much going wrong?"

Whenever two or more mothers get together, the conversation turns to a comparison of problems, or becomes a stream of complaints. The kinds of statements one hears are, "Adam is so obstinate, I can't make him do anything," "Gloria's whining drives me up the wall," or, "Give me a baby until he is crawling: after that you can take him."

If Hymes is right and children are fundamentally social, then in what way are parents thwarting the natural direction of their growth so that they become so thoroughly unsocial? The task of this book is to answer that question.

Before my first child was born, I read many books on child rearing. I found them to be bewilderingly contradictory. Until she was two, I related to my daughter in a hit and miss fashion with varying degrees of success and failure, just as most people do. Then I met my present husband. He introduced me to a fully integrated philosophy of living which could be applied to all aspects of interpersonal relationships. I found his ideas tremendously exciting. He had already realized that his system of beliefs could be applied to children, as well as adults, but having no children of his own, he had not refined it in detail. Together, we and some of our friends set about systematically applying the principles of this philosophy to our children.

The results were as exciting and rewarding as we ever hoped they would be. Living with our children now gives us all the fulfillment and pleasure most people only dream of. Minor problems arise from time to time, but they are no greater than those which develop in any mutually satisfying relationship. When they do arise, we ask ourselves where we have been inconsistent in applying our system. Invariably, we discover both the mistake and the solution.

2

The Adult Test

Most adults regard children as a completely different species from themselves. They have one way of behaving when they relate to other adults, and a totally different set of rules which they apply to children.

It is important to remember that children are people too. They are much smaller and weaker than we are, but women are usually smaller and weaker than men, and that is not a reason for treating them as inferior. Children have greater sleep needs and require more protein and calcium in their diet than we do because they are growing so fast; but different adults have different sleep and dietary needs, depending on their somatotype, and that does not make one less worthy of respect than another. Children only begin to realize that they are separate individuals somewhere around eight months, and take longer still to develop a clear time concept and to understand fully what death means; but it is experience which enables them to integrate these concepts, and it is experience which is the important difference between them and us.

Children are rational and logical, and want to be happy, just as we do.

Many people would disagree with this statement. They would argue that children are irrational and illogical and do not act in their own self-interest; however, if you examine these arguments, you will discover that what they are really saying is that children lack knowledge.

That which sets man apart from other animals is his rationality. That is to say that most of his actions are not instinctive, but are based on reason. Our children do not develop this ability to reason at some arbitrary age. They are born with it. Every new experience they have provides them with another opportunity to apply it.

Take the example of a tiny baby. He is born with a rooting reflex. He turns his head instinctively toward anything which touches his cheek. Thus, when held to the breast, he automatically turns toward the nipple and grasps it; however, within a short while, this reflex is replaced with a conscious action which results from his reason. He recognizes his mother by her appearance and smell. He learns that where she is, there is food. By the time he is seven months old, he will lean towards her breasts and pull at her clothing when he is hungry. He is now acting rationally and logically on the basis of his experience.

It is not irrational for a child to step on a piece of broken glass if he does not know that glass cuts. It is not irrational for him to refuse an injection intended for the purpose of inoculation if he does not understand what may happen if he is not inoculated. In other words, within the context of his experience, everything that a child does is based on reason, and is a logical consequence of what has gone before.

Children have thoughts, ideas, feelings, wants, and needs, just as we do; but they do not have the means to attain their ends. It is experience, and the knowledge that comes with it, which provides us with the tools for the pursuit of happiness. This is what children lack.

To compensate, they have an immense curiosity and an insatiable desire to learn. All their actions are aimed at gaining control of their lives and their environment. Every minute of every day, they are rapidly closing the experience gap. Our responsibility is to stand quietly by, always ready for an opportunity to help them reach their potential autonomy as fully as possible.

The Adult Test

The only important difference between adults and children is experience.

Try and imagine that your child is a fully grown person from an alien planet. He has the same mental and physical potential

If she breaks something by mistake, help her to clean up the mess in the same way you would help a friend.

as you, but is a "stranger in a strange land." Everything is new. He doesn't understand the mores of your culture. For example, he knows nothing about ownership or common courtesy. He has no knowledge of the properties of liquids or solids, or the effects of gravity. All these, and thousands of other things, must be learned. In addition, he is not yet physically adapted to deal properly with his environment. He lacks strength and simple skills. If you met such a person, you would, with dignity and courtesy, do everything possible to help him cope with his new world.

Once your child begins to communicate effectively, somewhere between ten months and two years, you should treat him in precisely the same way.

Whenever you are not sure how you should respond to your child's actions, apply the Adult Test. Ask yourself, "What would I do if this were an adult?"

In the following chapters, there are many examples of how the adult test should be applied. Here is one to begin with. If your friend visits your house and breaks a glass by mistake, do you shout "you clumsy idiot!" at her and shove her out of your way? On the contrary, you understand that she did not intend to break the glass, you allay her feelings of guilt and help her clean up the mess. If she broke the glass because she had never seen one before, and presumed that it would behave in the same way as a plastic tumbler, you might take a little time to point out the difference. You should relate to your child exactly as you would to your friend.

You need to get into the habit of applying the adult test to all your children's actions. That is the best and easiest way to help them take their places in society.

Summary

1. Children are rational and logical, within the context of their limited experience.

2. The only significant difference between adults and children is experience, and the knowledge that comes with it.

3. Making allowance for their lack of experience, we should treat children exactly as we treat adults.

3

Three Positions and a Fourth Alternative

Most people hold one of three fundamental attitudes which govern their relationships with their children. They are either authoritarian, permissive, or a mixture of the two.

The attitude of the authoritarian parents goes something like this: "I know best and my kids know nothing. I will decide everything for them. I know better than they what they should eat and what they should wear. I know what time they should go to sleep and for how long, what their interests should be, and exactly how they should behave; and God help them if they have any ideas of their own."

On the other hand, the permissive parent believes that he has no rights at all. His children can rampage through the home doing exactly as they wish and making endless demands. This parent believes he must respond to all the whims of his children and never say an angry word, in case he damages their vulnerable egos.

Both of these extreme positions have one virtue: the actions of the parents are partially predictable; but very few people are consistent. The authoritarian parent gives up in despair when his little boy has been staring mutinously, with a lump in his throat, at the same heap of spinach served up at all meals for two days, and still refuses to eat it. The permissive parent finally reaches the end of his tether when his daughter rushes through the living room, screeching at the top of her voice, for the fifth time, while he is trying to watch his favorite television program. She is carried screaming to her room and shut in there, only to be released some minutes later by a very repentant father.

The third position is occupied by parents who act indiscriminately, according to their present mood. The real horror of this in-between position is that the behavior of these parents is totally unpredictable. Their children have no consistent cause or effect in their lives. They live in a bewildering state of confusion, never knowing what the consequences of their actions will be. All they learn is that sometimes they are beaten, sometimes not. Sometimes they are ridiculed, sometimes loved; but there is no apparent logical reason for anything that happens. They go through life seeking to avoid unexpected pain, but never finding out how.

The Fourth Position

The authoritarian adult believes children have no rights. The permissive parent believes he himself has no rights. The in-between parent has no clear views at all. Happily there is a fourth alternative which is simple, logical, and easy for children to integrate.

The fourth position is one in which adults recognize that all people should have the same rights, regardless of age. The principle underlying this position is simply that every person should be entitled to live as he chooses, provided he does not harm other people or their property.

When this principle is applied to very young children, their lack of experience has to be taken into consideration. Naturally, they must be protected from basic dangers of which they can have no knowledge. They cannot be left to wander onto busy roads, drink bottles of turpentine, or eat cigarette butts. Apart from these obvious limitations, this principle can be applied consistently to children. If it is, they are quick to see how they benefit from it, and to understand why they should apply it themselves.

This book aims to show that, whenever conflict arises between adults and children (from toddlers to teenagers), it is because this principle is not understood and respected. Conversely, when it is applied consistently, the result is mutual freedom and respect.

Summary

1. Authoritarian parents believe their children have no rights.

2. Permissive parents believe they themselves have no rights.

3. "In-between" parents vacillate between the authoritarian and permissive positions.

4. There is a fourth alternative where parents recognize that both adults and children have rights, and that they can live in mutual respect and freedom.

4

The Basic Principle

Provided he does not harm other people or their property, every person should be free to act as he chooses.

Because of the great importance of this principle, we need to take time to consider exactly what it means before we apply it to child rearing.

The principle consists of two parts. The first concerns our respect for other people and their property; the second, our freedom to act as we choose. If you examine the meaning of these two parts, you will see that they are reverse sides of the same coin. One side of the coin is concerned with my freedom to live as I wish; the other with yours. The one cannot exist without the other. In other words, freedom can only exist where it is mutual.

What happens if someone violates the first part of the principle, and threatens you or your property? In this case, the use of force is justified to restore or protect freedom. If I compel you to go to church on Sunday, then I am violating your freedom; but if I stop you from hitting me or damaging my property, then I am protecting my freedom. I am acting in self-defense, and thus maintaining a state in which we are *both* free.

People often say that freedom is a meaningless concept because they are "forced" to do any number of things they would rather not do; but freedom does not mean only doing enjoyable things.

For example, I wash dishes, even though it is a task I dislike. I may say that I am "forced" to wash them because otherwise I will have no clean ones to eat from; but the truth is that I *choose* to wash them because I prefer them clean.

This chapter discusses briefly why the basic principle is fundamental to all positive interaction between parents and children. Let us first examine the first half of the statement:

Provided he does not harm other people or their property...

Societies would function extremely well if all people had complete respect for one another's lives and property. The common law of most societies is based to some extent on this belief. Theft, assault, arson, murder, and other violations of person and property are considered unacceptable in all but a few remote and primitive places. The tragedy is that, in this area more than any other, a double standard is applied to children.

All but the most permissive among us try to prevent our children from damaging our property and persons, but how many of us respect the lives and property of our children?

Children learn best by example and experience. If we want them to respect us, then we must respect them.

When an adult owns something, he can do whatever he likes with it, including destroying it. He expects that other people will ask his permission before they do anything to it.

A child, however, is told that if he does not play with his toys properly, they will be taken away. They are frequently discarded or passed on to other children without his permission. If he breaks them, he is punished and may even be beaten. Yet, he is expected to understand that he must not interfere with the property of others. There is no logical reason why he should understand this, since he never experiences the pride of total ownership himself, and children are, above all, logical.

Adults do not expect to be physically punished unless they commit a most heinous crime with foresight and intention. Even then, they usually have a lawyer to plead their case. Yet with children, corporal punishment is the order of the day. Extenuating circumstances are seldom considered, and they have no advocate, but they are expected to understand that they must never hit, bite, or scratch other people. Unless they know that no person will ever intentionally hurt them, how can they understand that they should not hurt others?

Your child will learn not to attack you physically or damage your possessions if you punish him every time he does so. Even if you beat him and don't let him own his own property, he will learn that, but the basis of his learning will be fear.

If, on the other hand, you respect his property and never assault him physically, then he will treat you the same way. He will have learned from your example, and his own experience, that you should "Do unto others as you would have them do unto you."

The chapters dealing with toys, clothing, and discipline will show in detail how parents can help their children grasp this all-important principle of mutual respect for property and person.

The second half of the basic principle must always be considered in the light of the first. It states:

...every person should be free to act as he chooses.

Human beings have a powerful built-in drive to control their lives and their environment. It is largely due to this drive that mankind has survived and flourished.

One only has to observe the untiring efforts of a baby in his first year to control his body to become aware of his urge for independence. He never tires of trying first to sit, then crawl, and later walk, run, and jump. He wants to brush his own hair, guide his own spoon to his mouth, and master the art of screwing and unscrewing bottle tops. He reaches endlessly for new objects to explore, manipulate, and control.

Anyone who has related to a two-year-old will have noticed the delight he takes in saying "no." He has found a powerful word with which to exercise his options.

When an adult tries to impose his will on a child, friction always results. Roy is determined to do up his shoe laces, even if it takes half an hour. Jenny wants to go swimming before she does her homework, regardless of what mother says. Andy can't see why he shouldn't go out on school nights. The list of things which children want to do against the wishes of their parents is endless. Every effort they make to decide for themselves what their actions should be is frustrated. Many eventually lapse into an apathetic state in which they simply follow instructions and completely lose the ability to make decisions. Others rebel uniformly against everything, in a desperate attempt to retain their autonomy.

On the whole, adults have far greater freedom than children to control their lives, but we are subject to many rules and regulations, too. The State plays a paternalistic role in our lives. It regulates us in diverse areas. For instance, it severely limits what we may buy and from whom, it takes and spends our money in the form of taxes, forces us to carry identity documents, and so on. Just as we tell our children that the rules which restrict them are in their interest, so the State assures us that its laws are for our own benefit; but ask any person if he thinks he can decide for himself what is good for him. The answer is always yes. It is only and always others we believe cannot look after themselves.

Most of us do not mind at all if an acquaintance explains at length why smoking is bad for us, but we do mind if he prevents us by force from buying a pack of cigarettes. Anybody may try to persuade us that we will be better off if we go to church on Sundays, but we would strongly resent being forced to go there. What is more, given all available information, more often than not, we do make those decisions which are right for our own needs, as we see them.

The reason adults tend to make the right decisions is that they want to be happy and are fundamentally rational. When they make mistakes, it is frequently because they have had so little experience in decision-making during childhood.

Thus, just as we want to be free to live our lives as we choose, so we should allow our children the freedom to live theirs as they see fit.

We can offer our children the information which we have and which they lack. We can tell them what course of action we believe will make them happiest, but in the end, all children grow up and must make their own decisions, and the more practice they have had in exercising their judgment as children, the easier it will be for them as adults. As John Holt says in *What Do I Do Monday?*: "It is *always* better, if he can do so at not too great a cost or risk, for a child to find out something for himself than to be told. Only from making choices and judgments can he learn to make them better, or learn to trust his own judgment."

Jenny will find out for herself that if she goes swimming before she does her homework, she will not have time to watch TV, or she will be too tired to work well, or she may not get around to doing her work at all and will then be in trouble at school. On the other hand, she may discover that she works well after a swim because she does so willingly and without resentment.

Even a newborn or small baby will be far more contented if you follow his cues. He already knows his needs better than you. Feed him when he is hungry. Cuddle him, or let him sleep or play when he shows you that that is what he wants. It is both easier and harder to impose your will on a tiny infant than on a child of any other age. There is nothing he can do to stop you making him wait another hour for his food. He cannot reason or cajole. When he wants to hear your voice or see your smile, he cannot prevent you from leaving him alone to cry because you think he should sleep. On the other hand, there are few people who can bear to listen to the desperate and frantic cries of a baby whose needs are not being fulfilled. At this stage, he bears no malice, nor is he calculating, and his consciousness is too primitive for him to understand that you, too, have needs.

While your young crawler or toddler is still too young to understand that he can damage or be damaged by things, give him all the freedom you can by simply removing them from his reach. Shouting "no" or smacking a baby who doesn't understand your reason accomplishes nothing except his frustration, distress, and mistrust. It teaches him that sometimes his actions are met with smiles, sometimes with anger, and that these reactions are arbitrary and irrational. Far better to make sure the stairs have a gate, top and bottom, the swimming pool a fence, and that poisonous or breakable objects are well out of reach.

However, it is surprising how early a baby can grasp simple concepts. Your one-year-old will quickly learn what heat is if you touch a teapot briefly and then pull your hand away sharply saying "hot!" and then hold his hand close to the pot, so that he can feel the heat.

Let your baby hold his hand close to a tea pot and feel the heat while you repeat the word "hot." That way he will learn what "hot" means without hurting himself.

When my first daughter was eleven months old, she put her hand on an asbestos heater, despite warnings, and got a fright, though the heat was not sufficient to burn her. For several days afterwards, she only had to glance at the heater or hear the word "hot" to burst into tears. She never again touched anything I told her was hot.

From two years on, children rapidly become capable of making more and more of their own day-to-day decisions.

The idea of children being free to decide for themselves what they should eat, or wear, or do, or when they should sleep and for how long, fills most people with horror. They make dire and gloomy predictions about the chaos which would inevitably result.

This book aims to show that quite the opposite is true. Children who live in mutual freedom with their families are responsible and self-disciplined, and learn quickly to do what is in their self-interest.

Summary

1. Freedom cannot exist between a parent and child unless it is mutual.

2. Force is only acceptable when it is used to protect or restore freedom; that is, when it is used in self-defense or in the defense of another person or their property.

3. People always act freely, unless someone stops them from doing so by force, or the threat of force.

4. Children learn by example, so if we want them to respect us, we must respect them.

5. Children learn by experience, so when it is safe, they should make all their own decisions, and be allowed to learn from their mistakes.

6. Children have a powerful drive to control their environment. Every time we interfere with this drive, we create a conflict.

5

"In Arms," Separation, and Diet

If a child is emotionally secure and physically healthy, the methods described in this book will be easy to implement, and astonishingly successful. If he has been deprived of early physical contact, or suffers from separation anxiety, or has an inadequate diet, they will not work nearly as well.

For this reason, although these three issues are discussed in depth elsewhere, and although they are not central to the freedom principle, they must be dealt with briefly now.

The "In-arms" Period

Small babies are little bundles of needs. They need to have full tummies, plenty of sleep, and above all, lots of cuddling. They know only their immediate feelings. They cannot think ahead. They cannot understand that, though they are hungry now, feeding time is not for another hour; or that, though they are lonely now, Mother is busy and will attend to them later. All they know is that they are experiencing pain, and nothing is being done about it.

It is only in our highly developed culture that babies spend so much time alone in cribs, strollers, baby chairs, push-chairs, and numerous other carrying devices. Babies in most primitive societies, and the infants of all other mammals, are in close contact with their mothers until they are able to move away alone. Only in our society have bizarre ideas developed about babies being "spoiled" by too much attention. Actually, the converse is true. We do our babies great harm when we leave them alone to cry, make them wait in misery for their food, and hardly ever hold them or cuddle them.

Psychiatrists and social workers have recently become aware of the tremendous importance of early physical contact. Babies in institutions who are fed and changed, but not talked to or held and cuddled, are listless and apathetic. In extreme cases, they have been known to die for no other reason than deprivation of love. In all cases, their development is severely retarded; they sit, talk, and crawl very late, and have abnormally low IQs.

In *The Continuum Concept*, Jean Liedloff describes how the babies of the Yequana Indians, who are "in-arms" constantly from birth until they can crawl, are happy and alert. They hardly ever cry, and Ms. Liedloff did not see a single case of thumb-sucking. The Yequana mothers carry their babies all the time, sleeping and waking. The infants sleep with their mothers at night and are breast fed until they lose interest.

Give your baby as much physical contact as you can. If possible, breast feed her. Breast feeding, apart from its convenience and nutritional superiority, is the best way of providing your baby with the feelings of warmth, security, and of being loved that she needs. If you bottle-feed, hold the baby close, just as you would if she were at the breast.

Do not leave your baby to cry. No good comes of it. Moore and Ucko[1] have found that the infants who wake most in the early months are those whose parents do not go to them immediately when they wake and cry, for fear of "spoiling" them. They also discovered that babies between six and nine months who woke at night and cried were usually those who received little attention and were left to cry in the day.

In *Babyhood*, Penelope Leach points out that many mothers, and the people who advise them, believe that it is acceptable for babies to cry only if there is something physically wrong with

1. Penelope Leach, *Babyhood*.

them. If a baby's diaper is chafing or she is hungry, for instance, then she is justified in crying, and it is her mother's duty to attend to the problem; but if the baby is crying out of loneliness or boredom, then she should be left to "cry it out." Desire for human company is not considered a valid reason for distress, despite the fact that mental stimulation and social relationships are necessary for the infant's normal development.

Ms. Leach goes on to observe that we do not treat adults in the same way: "We do not reckon that a husband who has been given his supper 'should not' require anything more of us until morning. Nor do we greet friends on the telephone by saying, 'Do you actually need me to do anything for you? Because if not, I am going to hang up.' A chat is a valid reason for the telephone call." (p. 209).

I am not suggesting that you must carry your baby all the time as is done in some primitive cultures. Although this may be ideal, it is not practical in our culture. First of all, most of us are not strong enough, since we have not been carrying babies on our backs from an early age. Secondly, the way we live makes it impossible. It may be that the time our infants spend happily playing with toys and looking at mobiles is in fact beneficial, in that it prepares them to cope intellectually with our life-style, but never leave your baby to cry. Don't make her wait for her meals. Cuddle her as much as you can, and walk her, rock her, and soothe her to sleep when she needs it.

The Continuum Concept contends that when children are deprived of early physical contact, they suffer from a sense of alienation which remains with them for life, and stunts every aspect of their development. Conversely, the in-arms experience leads to independence and emotional maturity. The child can only become truly autonomous if her early needs for closeness and dependence have been fulfilled.

Separation

Separation anxiety is directly related to deprivation of the in-arms experience in the sense that they are both problems of sep-

Carry your baby as much as you can. Physical contact makes him feel
happy and contented.

aration; however, even if a baby has a good early relationship
with her mother, the effects of lengthy separation from her between
the age of about one month and three years will still be traumatic
and long-lasting. If it is at all possible, you should try never to
leave your child prior to the age of three for longer than she can
accept without indicating distress.

In his book *Separation: Anxiety and Anger,* John Bowlby described the effects of separation on the child, and the typical sequence of behavior which occurs whenever a child is separated from his mother or a substitute to whom he has become attached.

The child is at first extremely distressed and "tries by all means available to him to recover his mother." His distress is more or less intense, depending on the relative familiarity or strangeness of his new environment and the people caring for him. Next, the child seems to lose hope of recovering his mother, but nevertheless remains preoccupied with her and continues to watch for her return. Finally, he appears to give up hope entirely and lose all interest in his mother. Provided the child is not separated from his mother for too long, his attachment for her will re-emerge; after that, for a long time, he will cling to her and become very upset if she should show any sign of leaving again.

Bowlby explains that the same behavior in the child also results from emotional absence of the mother. If the mother is with the child physically, but withdraws from him emotionally, or rejects him as a result of depression or preoccupation with other matters, or threatens to abandon him as a form of punishment, the child experiences the same distress as he would from physical separation.

Various studies have shown that small children explore with confidence and courage if their mothers are present, but become fearful and withdrawn in their absence.

Monkeys are similar to humans in both their attachment and separation behavior. Experiments on the effects of one or two weeks' separation of monkey babies from their mothers can therefore be viewed with interest. It has been found that when a monkey baby is separated from his mother, he undergoes a period of extreme distress, followed by apathy and inactivity. After being reunited with his mother, there is a marked increase in the baby's clinging, and in some cases, tantrums occur when the mother rejects the baby.

In one such study, monkeys were separated from their mothers for six days when they were about twenty weeks old. At the age of thirty months, they still showed signs of disturbed behavior, less locomotor activity, and less social play. They were also more timid and less adventurous than monkeys who had not experienced separation.

Separation anxiety occurs when a mother leaves her child for only a few days. It also results from mothers going to work, or from a child being sent to nursery school before he is ready. Bowlby has discovered that the longer the separation, the worse and more prolonged are the effects.

There are mitigating factors, however. The effects on the child are less traumatic if his relationship with his mother is good, if he is left with an effective mother-substitute (for example a grandmother he knows well), if he has a companion (sibling or other) whom he knows well, and if he is in familiar surroundings. So if you have to leave your child, perhaps to go to the hospital, leave him with his father or someone he knows very well, preferably in his own home.

By the time they are three years old, children are able to understand that their mothers will return, and by four years there is seldom any problem at all. Bowlby concludes from his investigations that prior to three, "the safe dose of separation is no dose."

Diet

There is no question that inadequate diet has a significant effect on human behavior. Deficiencies of certain vitamins and minerals, and insufficient quantities of proteins, fats, and carbohydrates affect every part of the body. The results are vast and varied. They commonly include listlessness, depression, hyperactivity, irritability, and hyper-sensitivity.

In *Let's Have Healthy Children,* Adelle Davis writes that malnutrition is a common phenomenon among American children of all classes. In many cases, their staple diet consists largely of refined bread and rice, sweets, soft drinks, and potato chips. Consequently, they are perpetually ill with various infections, allergies, and viruses.

Hyperactivity has become such a serious problem in North America that as many as thirty percent of all children are given drugs to control their behavior. In addition to damaging the liver and destroying many nutrients, these drugs are addictive. According to Ms. Davis, most hyperactive children would be completely cured by an adequate diet.

Adelle Davis also discusses tests in which improved nutrition greatly benefited autistic children. She points out that, if a pregnant woman has an inadequate diet, and her baby's nutrition is poor after birth as well, he will very likely suffer from adrenal exhaustion, which causes colic, eczema, stubborn diaper rash, and later, ". . . such a child craves sweets and becomes a rebellious underachiever at school, lacks the ability to concentrate, is subject to periods of excessive tiredness, and is characterized by emotional immaturity" (p. 110).

How to ensure that your child eats an adequate diet with a healthy appetite is discussed in the chapter on feeding. Those foods which are necessary to make a balanced diet are listed in any number of other books.

Conclusion

If your child is suffering the consequences of in-arms deprivation, separation anxiety, or poor diet, the ideas in this book will still work better than any other method of child-rearing, but the results will not be nearly as gratifying as they would without these problems.

Start by improving your child's diet—that is relatively easy and straightforward. If she is insecure and clingy, or unhappy and rebellious due to separation anxiety or lack of physical contact in the first few months of her life, then give her all the attention you can. It is no good telling your clinging child to stop being a baby and grow up. Let her stay close to you, give her all the attention and cuddles possible. Consider allowing her to sleep in your bed. Make sure the separation is not repeated. Gradually and in time, her confidence and sense of security will return.

Supplementary Reading

The Continuum Concept by Jean Liedloff
The Womanly Art of Breast Feeding La Leche League Manual
Touching by Ashley Montagu
Separation: Anxiety and Anger by John Bowlby
Let's Have Healthy Children by Adelle Davis
Babyhood by Penelope Leach

6

Independence, Individuality, and Self-Esteem

There are very many reasons why people have children. Some of us have them by choice, others by mistake. One couple has as many as possible because they need workers to help in the fields or the house, or bring extra money into the home. Other parents hope their children will fulfill their own failed ambitions. One mother wants her daughter to be a ballet dancer or beauty queen, another hopes hers will become an eminent lawyer or take over her father's business. Some people simply want their children to excel in every way, so that they can bask in their reflected glory. There are a few who have children to satisfy religious and patriotic values.

Many of us simply hope to derive pleasure from watching our children grow and develop, and from their companionship. We hope they will be happy people with fulfilling lives. This attitude is the one most likely to benefit both our children and ourselves.

The three main qualities you need to foster in your child's personality are independence, self-esteem, and individuality.

These three attributes are essential if he is to be happy, fulfilled, and a good companion. If the relationships in your family are governed by the fundamental principles of mutual freedom and respect, then these qualities will develop automatically in your children. Unfortunately, in many homes, they seem to be the traits which parents are most determined to destroy.

Independence

Gwen believes her children should do things for themselves, but she washes and dries them when they take a bath. She hangs their clothes up for them, and dresses them. She drives to school in the middle of the morning with their books and lunch if they forget them. She blows their noses and wipes their bottoms. How can they gain these skills if they never get a chance to practice them?

The only advantage of doing everything for your children is that it saves time in the short run. In the long run, it wastes far more time than it ever saves, robs them of self-confidence, and breeds dependence. It is unfortunate that so many mothers rely for their own sense of self-worth on a feeling of being needed. These are the same mothers who like tiny babies best "because they are so totally dependent and helpless."

Allow your children to do as much as possible, and never underestimate their abilities. They start off with a tremendous drive for efficacy and independence. It takes several years of hard work to annihilate it and produce a pathetic creature whose standard response to any challenge is, "I can't."

All children who are not physically or mentally disabled can wash and dry themselves, dress themselves, hang up their clothes, use a knife and fork, pour drinks, carry breakable objects, and many other simple everyday actions by the age of three, if they are given a chance and shown how.

Help your child to become independent by scaling down all the furniture in his room to his size. That way he will have no trouble reaching anything. Make a box or get him a little chair he can carry around so that he can reach light switches, door knobs, lavatory seats, drawers, shelves, and so on. Show him how to blow his own nose, do up buttons, shoe laces, and zippers, polish his shoes, sweep the floor, mop up messes, pour fluids, and so on. Consult *Montessori in the Home* for ways in which to help your child become independent. Small children love learning to control their environment.

The Yequana Indians of South America do nothing which will curb their children's independence. In *The Continuum Concept*, Jean Liedloff describes an incident concerning a boy of nine, called Tadehah, whom she took with her on an expedition up-river because she was filming and he was particularly photogenic.

In the course of the expedition, there was a disagreement and Tadehah's tribesmen suddenly decided to return home. As they were leaving, they called out to the boy to join them—to which he quietly replied, "No."

The men made no effort to change his mind. They simply accepted his decision to stay with three total strangers, far from home, as "an expression of his self-ownership."

Leidloff says: "Among the Yequana, a person's judgment is thought to be adequate to make any decision he feels motivated to make. The impulse to make a decision is evidence of the ability to do it suitably; small children do not make large decisions; they are strongly interested in self-preservation, and in matters beyond their comprehension, they look to elders to judge what is best."

Thus, these children become accustomed to making decisions from a very early age, and seldom make mistakes.

A cousin of mine told me of how he wanted to go into the city alone when he was nine years old. His parents were somewhat fearful for his safety, but decided that his independence was more important than their fears. They suggested that he work out how much money he would need for his bus fares, for whatever purchases he might want to make, and for possible phone calls. The money he used was his own. They also advised him to make a note of any phone number he might need. Thus prepared, he set out on his adventure. He eventually arrived home, none the worse for his experience and feeling very pleased with himself. He remains proud of that independence to this day.

By the time your children are teenagers, they should be making all their own decisions, only turning to you for consultation or discussion. Remember that, until this century, teenagers both worked for their livings and supported and raised families successfully. In pre-industrial Europe, by the time a boy was eight, he was expected either to leave home or, if he stayed, to be self-sufficient.

Self-esteem

Many psychologists now accept that people need self-esteem more than any other quality in order to be happy. A person with self-esteem likes being himself. He feels confident and capable of running his own life. He does not suffer from insecurity, jealousy, or feelings of inadequacy. He feels that he is a person of worth.

Little babies take quite a while to become aware that they are separate from the world around them. Gradually, they begin to perceive a difference between people and inanimate objects, and then to realize that they themselves are separate, too. Somewhere around two years, they become completely aware of their individuality, but long before that, they begin to build up a self-image. Initially, this image is entirely a reflection of how they are seen by the people around them. If a baby is cuddled and loved, and his smiles are responded to with joy, he gets a feeling of being worthwhile and wanted. As he grows older, his own ability begins to affect his self-image too. This is when it becomes so important to let him do as much as possible for himself, so that he can take pride in being able to control his world to some extent.

Jimmy is two years old. When his mother sees him setting off across the room with a bowl of water, she says, "Put that down at once, you're going to spill all over the floor!" A command like this does very little to improve Jimmy's self-image. Instead, his mother might say, "Look, darling, that water is spilling because the bowl is so full. If you pour some water into the sink first, and walk very carefully keeping the bowl level like this, then you will be able to carry it without spilling." She could give her son a cloth and show him how to wipe up any water spilled. This way, he would get the idea that he can do things, rather than that he cannot.

In *Between Parent and Child,* Haim Ginott says, "Labeling is disabling." It is indeed very destructive to self-esteem. When Jemima runs through the house and bangs into a chair, her mother raises her eyebrows and sighs. The next time they are visiting friends, she says in front of Jemima, "Oh, Jemima is a real clumsy clutz. I'm going to have to pay for ballet classes to try and make her more graceful." Apart from the fact that, from now on, Jemima will probably always believe that she is clumsy, such a remark is extremely ill-mannered. Jemima's mother would never say that about another adult in her presence. If she really believes that her child has a serious problem, which is unlikely since children normally lack coordination, she could arrange for her to go to ballet classes without giving clumsiness as a reason.

In *The Continuum Concept,* Jean Liedloff points out that adults respond to destructive or antisocial behavior in children as if it is to be expected, with "a hopeless shrug, a blanket indictment like 'Boys will be boys'." The implication is that "bad-ness is solidly built in."

If, on the other hand, the child does something which demonstrates independence, or creativity, or thoughtfulness, the reaction among adults is one of surprise. Startled exclamations of praise indicate to the child that the social behavior he has shown is "unexpected, uncharacteristic, and unusual."

If you tell your children often enough that they are stupid, clumsy, or incapable, your words and deeds may prove to be a self-fulfilling prophecy. Your children may well become just as stupid, clumsy, or incapable as you tell them they are.

Children who lack self-confidence soon stop trying. They feel, "Well, I can't do anything right, so it's not worth bothering any more." This attitude, besides making them pretty hard to live with, can handicap them for life.

If you want to comment on your child's behavior, describe the action that pleases or displeases you. Don't label the child. Try to reinforce good behavior rather than bad.

For example, when Carol's mother had a friend around to tea, Carol was very courteous. She said "please" and "thank you," and "excuse me" when she needed to interrupt the conversation. When the friend was leaving, she said to Carol's mother, "What delightful manners your child has!" That night Carol's mother said to her, "When Mrs. M. was going home, she told me how she enjoyed meeting a little girl with such good manners." From that time on, Carol took great pride in her politeness.

By the time they are three to four years old, children begin to respond to the reactions of their peer group, as well as that of their parents. It becomes important to them that they are accepted by others of their own age. This peer group influence grows stronger as they get older. Your children will be far less upset by the criticism of others, and much more able to stand up for their own beliefs and values, if they have high self-esteem.

We seriously damage our children's self-confidence when we continually discount their thoughts and feelings. What miraculous change takes place around eighteen to twenty years of age that makes us feel that someone is now worthy of respect? People don't need to accumulate experience in order to have thoughts and feelings. If you take your children's thoughts and feelings seriously, not only will they feel worthy of respect, but they will accord the same dignity to you.

When Andy comes in crying with a scratch on his knee, Gwen says to him, "What a baby you are! That little scratch doesn't hurt at all!" But when her husband comes in limping and explains that he banged his shin on the car door, she does not dream of dismissing his pain so cursorily.

When Jenny comes to her mother and says, "Mom, did you know that God is a giant with a big black beard who lives in the sun?" her mother smiles indulgently and says to her friend sitting by, "Aren't these kids cute with the funny ideas they pick up?" Imagine how her husband would react if she responded in the same way to his latest theory on the rising cost of living!

If you do not want your children to think that they are fools and not worthy of consideration, take them seriously; allow them some dignity, too. Recognize that the "silly" things they say are perfectly sensible, given their present limited knowledge. If you correct and add to their information, their conclusions will be at least as reliable as an adult's.

Individuality

There is nothing more precious to a human being of self-esteem than his own individuality. We all like to feel that we are different from anyone else. When we fall in love, part of our pleasure is derived from the feeling that "here is someone who knows all my personality traits, mannerisms, and habits, and values them because they are unique."

Enjoy watching your children's personalities develop; don't type-cast them by deciding when they are in the cradle what they are like. Do something by doing nothing. Stand aside and let them be.

This is not always easy. Right from the beginning, babies differ from one another. This baby cries little and sleeps a lot. This one seems interested in the world around, but quickly becomes fretful. It is a temptation to decide when your baby is only three months old that he is going to have a placid nature, or that he will become a musician because he has long fingers, or a football player because he kicks so hard. It is especially dangerous when a parent sees his children as a means of fulfilling his own unrequited ambitions.

We put children in boxes and label them "sensitive and temperamental," "hard-working and methodical," "sweet and ladylike," and so on. We decide "David will be a top lawyer," "Mary is so artistic, she is sure to become a painter," "Jane is a born teacher." There may well be truth in our observations, but give children the chance to decide for themselves.

All her life, Judith's parents pointed to her mathematical abilities. She fulfilled their prophecy and became a computer programmer. Only in her thirties did she become conscious of a desire to investigate other fields. She was lucky and able to return to the university and study speech and hearing therapy. A whole new world opened up to her. Another person of less self-esteem and less financial security might never have taken the opportunity to break into new and more fulfilling areas.

Mary-Anne grew up being told that her talents lay in the sciences, her sister was the artistic one of the family. She never tried her hand at drawing or painting because she was firmly convinced that she had no ability. When she was forty, she was persuaded, with some difficulty, to attend an art class with a friend. She found that, not only did she derive great pleasure from painting, but she was good at it, too.

All his life, Gary was told what a good boy he was. "Gary is the boy who was born on the Sabbath day," his mother would say, "bonny and blithe, good and gay." In his late teens, Gary started breaking all the rules. He dropped out, smoked pot, and rebelled against everything and everyone. Later he said, "I was so tired of being called 'good.' I realize now that I simply needed to show my parents that I had a mind of my own."

We all, to some extent, encourage our sons and daughters to fit into the stereotyped patterns of behavior which are generally considered appropriate to their gender. Certain qualities of masculinity and femininity, such as grace in women and physical strength in men, are useful; but most of the positive qualities that are associated with either sex are equally attractive in the other.

A man is no less masculine for possessing such qualities as gentleness, sensitivity, and intuition, which are normally associated with women. A woman can be strong, assertive, independent, and decisive, and still be very feminine.

Sex stereotyping is just as dangerous as any other form of categorizing. There is no reason why your boys should not cry sometimes and be cuddled if they want it. Your daughters don't need to be pampered and protected from the world. They, too, are capable of great things. When you buy toys for your children, remember that your sons derive considerable pleasure and benefit from dolls and tea sets, stringing beads, crocheting, or cooking. By the same token, your daughters may thoroughly enjoy woodworking and mechanical things.

Don't have stereotyped expectations of your children. Your son may enjoy cooking, too.

It is easier to respect your children's individuality if you also respect your own. Before you had children, you had many other interests and activities. Once children arrive on the scene, they become an important part of your interests, but it is a mistake to let them become your whole life. It is far too great a burden for your children to bear if all your hopes and ambitions revolve around them, and they are the cause of all your joys and sorrows.

They need to know that you are interested in them and care about them, without their feeling responsible for your personal happiness. By the same token, you should not feel responsible for their ups and downs. Let them be. Don't fuss like a mother hen over every ailment. Don't get in a state when they tell you, "No one wants to play with me," or "Johnny scribbled in my book and tramped on my crayons at school today." They must cope with these problems alone, and a distressed parent is just an added burden.

Make it clear to your children that you have your own life to live, and that you need time to yourself to follow your personal interests, just as they do. If they understand that your individuality must be respected, they will appreciate it more when you respect theirs.

Summary

1. The three main qualities you need to encourage in your child's personality are independence, self-esteem, and individuality.
2. In order for children to be independent, they should do as much for themselves as possible, and make all their own decisions.
3. You will help build your children's self-esteem if you don't label them or discount their feelings. You should treat them with respect and courtesy, as you would a friend.
4. Don't type-cast your children. Let them grow and develop, each in his own direction.

Supplementary Reading
Your Child's Self-Esteem by D. Corkille Briggs

7

Food, Feeding, and Freedom

When Jenny was eleven months old, her mother, Gwen, had pretty strong ideas about what her baby should eat. She said to me one day, "Jenny won't eat anything that is good for her. I've even tried holding her nose and forcing porridge down her throat, but she gags and spits it up. She seems to be deliberately thwarting me." At meal times, Jenny would clamp her jaws together and turn her head sharply away as the spoon came for her mouth. She would grab for the spoon and knock it away, so that food spilled all over the floor. In desperation, Gwen tied her hands down. Still, Jenny refused to eat.

By the time Jenny was four, Gwen had resorted to persuasion as an alternative to force. One would hear "Chuff-chuff-chuff, whoo, whoo — here comes the chucca train, open your mouth so it can leave passengers at the station..." as Gwen tried to tempt a spoon of mashed potato into her daughter's mouth. By this time, the child existed almost exclusively on cornflakes and jelly.

Why is this kind of situation so familiar, when not only is the desire to eat a necessary survival instinct, but most people find food thoroughly enjoyable, too?

Children Know What Food Is Best for Them

The reason is that parents believe they know better than their children what and how much they should eat. They are sure that, if a child is left to decide for herself, she will waste away or get too fat, have a completely unbalanced diet or establish bad eating habits. The contrary is true. Children will eat an excellent diet with a healthy appetite, if they are given total freedom to eat whatever they like and as much as they want, with only one proviso: that junk food is not made readily available to them.

Babies love to eat. When they suck, they do so with total absorption. It is probably no exaggeration to say that, in the first few weeks of their lives, sucking is their greatest pleasure. No hungry baby will refuse food, and he knows exactly when he has had enough. If a breast-fed baby is allowed to drink as often and as long as she wants, she will establish a good supply of milk and gain weight steadily. A bottle-fed baby is equally capable of deciding when she wants more and when she has had enough. All these little ones need is a relaxed and loving atmosphere in which to savor the experience.

Most people, even when they accept that babies know instinctively how much milk they need, worry that things will go wrong when solids are introduced.

In *Baby and Child Care*, Dr. Spock describes certain experiments conducted by Clara Davis which demonstrate that these fears are groundless.

Dr. Davis wanted to find out what small children would eat if they were left to follow their natural appetites. For her experiment, she chose three babies, all between eight months and a year in age, who had been fed nothing but breast milk up to that time.

At mealtimes, these babies were allowed to choose from a smorgasbord of wholesome foods including vegetables, fruit, dairy products, wholegrain cereals, meat, fruit juices, and water.

The nurses who tended the babies were told not to influence the children in any way, and to help them only if they indicated a desire for a particular food and were unable to manage alone.

The eating patterns which developed from this experiment would horrify the average mother. Sometimes, the babies would binge on certain foods — for instance, they might drink up to a quart of milk with one meal and none at the next. One baby ate six hard boiled eggs, in addition to a full meal, on several occasions. They would eat nothing but fruit and vegetables for a while, and then only carbohydrates or proteins. Their appetites varied greatly from one meal to the next, and in general their meals were far from what is commonly understood by "well-balanced."

Nonetheless, none of the babies vomited or had upset tummies, and they all grew very well and were healthy by any standards. A record was kept of what each baby ate, and over a period of time it was found that they all had an excellent diet.

Dr. Davis concluded that when a baby needed a specific nutrient, he or she would concentrate on the food which supplied the nutrient until the need was met, then change to something else.

She later repeated the experiment with older children, including hospital patients, and the results were just as impressive.

A similar exercise was carried out in the 1930s, in an American orphanage. John Nicholson describes this experiment in *Habits*. In this case, a number of children were allowed to choose freely from a wide variety of foods for a period of six years. The children varied in age from newly weaned babies upward. Again, an effort was made not to influence their decisions in any way. These children, too, chose a completely adequate diet for themselves, and were exceptionally healthy. A few entered the orphanage with rickets, but they soon found cod liver oil among the foods offered, and drank it till they were cured.

The staff always knew a child was becoming ill because she would stop eating. Similarly, she would resume eating the day before she recovered.

I Can Feed Myself

Around the age of six months seems to be a good time to start introducing solids into a baby's diet. At this age, babies are putting everything into their mouths anyway, and many of them are starting to imitate the people around them. You can offer your baby a variety of finger foods from the family diet, for instance slices of apple, a wholewheat rusk, pieces of cheese or banana, or a chicken bone. She can also start playing with a spoon, and even trying to feed herself soft foods with it. In *Babyhood*, Penelope

Let your toddler prepare her own snacks, and she will soon handle utensils competently.

Leach says, "Some infants, who have been given the chance, can feed themselves completely by nine months."

Parents should not allow themselves to become anxious about food. Children very quickly become aware of their parents' concern. Eating should not become a moral issue, nor should food be used as a bribe. If none of these things happen, you may be sure that your children will welcome their meals with a healthy appetite.

Junk Foods

Many people argue that you cannot apply the adult test to children and let them eat what they like because, given the chance, they will eat nothing but junk food.

When Marion's godchild, seven-year-old Karen, came to stay for two weeks, her mother said to Marion, "I must warn you, the child doesn't eat a thing. She picks at her food like a bird. See how thin she is!" When Karen wandered in clutching the sticky remains of a chocolate bar, she added, "Anything she eats is better than nothing."

A week later, Karen came running into the kitchen, her face flushed with exertion, calling, "What's for lunch Aunty Marion, I'm starving!" She gobbled down a large plate of fish fingers, salad, and wholemeal bread, and finished off her meal with fruit and milk.

What brought about this miraculous change? Marion didn't have any junk food in her home. If her kids were hungry or thirsty between meals, they helped themselves to fruit, nuts, or raisins, milk or juice, or even the unmentionable—water! For the first time in her life, Karen didn't eat biscuits and sweets, or drink sugary beverages on and off all day. Into the bargain, she had the example of other children with unspoiled appetites to follow. Perhaps most important, nobody cared how much or how little she ate. She was under no pressure to live up to expectations or prove a point.

Nobody wants their child to live solely on junk foods, and certainly, if such foods are nibbled between meals, they are lethal to a healthy appetite; but if your child is eating rubbish, the question to ask is, where is she finding it? In her own home? If she is hungry or thirsty between meals and fancies a snack, she will settle for something nutritious if no sweets, cakes, chips, or soft drinks are available.

She will follow your example, too. If you eat junk, so will she. The answer is to have only wholesome food in your home, and make sure your own eating habits are good.

A problem does arise when your child goes to other people's houses and parties. There, you cannot control what food is available. You may fear that she will stuff herself with empty foods at every opportunity because that is what her friends eat,or because she doesn't get them at home.

You can make a point of explaining to your child why you eat nutritious foods, and why you think she should, too. Explain how different parts of the body are built with different kinds of food. A good way to help her understand this is by pinning up a picture of a child the same size as she is on her wall. Glue pictures of different types of nutritious foods around it, with arrows pointing to the parts of the body they help to build; or perhaps after your child has had some milk, she can stick a picture of milk on herself with arrows pointing to the teeth, hair, and bones. Carrots can be connected to the eyes, yogurt to the tummy, fruit to the skin, and so on. You can point out that sweets do not build anything except cavities. This is very simplistic, but it helps small children understand the connection between good food and healthy bodies.

With a very small child, you can simply tell her that junk food will spoil her teeth and make her ill. Don't go on about it too much, as it may then become the "forbidden fruit." Once you have made your simple explanation, when junk food is available, let her decide for herself what she will eat. If she has money to spend and wants to buy sweets and chips, don't stop her. Remember that, if your child's basic diet at home is good, a little junk food now and then will not do much harm. You may be pleasantly surprised by her self-control, as she will be strongly influenced by your example.

So far, we have discussed your child's freedom where food is concerned. Now let us look at the other side of the coin—that is, her respect for your rights.

Good Manners

Few adults like to sit at the table with children who make a mess all over the place, chew loudly, use their fingers, and never say please or thank you. There is no reason why they should. The dining room belongs to the parents, and they are entitled to enjoy pleasant mealtimes there; however, if children eat alone, they will not learn to eat properly because they will have no example to follow.

Children, from babies up, love to eat with the family. Let them eat with you, at least at breakfast and lunch times. From about eighteen months on, when a reasonable standard can be expected, teach them to eat properly. Point out that, when we eat with other people, we chew with a closed mouth, we don't throw our food on the floor, we say please and thank you, and so on. If your children persist in playing with their food and making more mess than necessary, they can be told that they must eat in the kitchen until they are ready to try and eat properly. By the time they are four, your children should have excellent table manners.

Whose Food Is It, Anyway?

You must decide clearly in your own mind to whom the food in your house belongs. If you regard all the food in your home as your property, then your children must be told this and they must ask permission for anything they want to eat. I find it easier to make ordinary staple foods freely available to the whole family; but I expect to be asked for certain special things such as cashew nuts, fruit cake, or out-of-season fruit which is expensive. I simply say, "Please ask me if you want some cherries." If your children take something they shouldn't without permission, they should compensate you. Compensation is dealt with in the chapter on discipline. If your children buy food with their own money, you should never take any of it without their permission.

Allowing your children the freedom to eat what they choose does not mean you should let them ask for five different things in a row, take one bite out of each and then discard the rest. Your child should eat what she has asked for before she is permitted something else, unless she is trying the food for the first time. If she is eating food which you have paid for, you are entitled to prevent her from wasting it.

When children are ill, they become cranky, irritable, and difficult to reason with. If you follow the methods outlined in this chapter, your children will be healthy, eat almost anything, and be on their way to becoming as happy and reasonable as you would like them to be.

Summary

1. If children are free to choose what they eat, they will have an excellent diet and a healthy appetite.

2. If you do not want your child to eat junk food, explain why it is bad for her, do not make it readily available, and do not eat it yourself.

3. It is your right to expect good manners at your table. Your child will learn them more easily if she watches you.

4. Decide which food in your home your children must ask for, and which they may take freely.

8

Toilet "Training"

Toilet training is an issue which looms large in many mothers' lives. When it is handled incorrectly, all kinds of problems result. Children become obstinate in their refusal to use the potty. They continue wetting and messing in their pants much longer than necessary. After they have been trained, they may relapse and start bed-wetting at a later stage. Often, they develop chronic constipation as a result of guilty feelings about their excretory processes that stay with them for life; but you can allow your child freedom to control his life in this area, too.

The whole concept of toilet "training" needs to be questioned. Dogs have to be "trained" to excrete outside. If we want a monkey to eat with a knife and fork, we need to train it; but children have a cognitive faculty. They learn by thought and imitation. They do not have to be "trained" to do anything. They merely need to be shown how to do things.

In the same way that your child will learn to feed herself by watching you, so she will learn to use the potty or lavatory by observation.

Children do not have an innate need to be contrary; they want to conform to the standards of those around them.

I have several friends whose children used a potty in a perfectly acceptable manner from somewhere around the age of two without any "training." I experienced the same thing with my daughter Justine. When she indicated that she knew she was going to have a bowel movement or to urinate by mentioning it to me, I recognized that she was now ready to control the process. I then directed her attention to the potty. She had seen people using lavatories many times. Once she had decided she wanted to use the potty, I took off her diapers and put her in training pants. Within a couple of weeks, she was using the potty all the time.

Accept that urinating and defecating are normal, healthy processes. There is nothing dirty, naughty, bad, or unacceptable about them. Once your children are old enough, they will quickly learn to do them in the right place, just as they learn to do many other more difficult things which society requires of them.

If your child has lapses and makes a mess in her pants from time to time, shouting at her or hitting her will certainly not help her to gain normal control. It will just fill her with fear, and might result in further mistakes, or constipation, or bed-wetting.

Many people have "hang-ups" about excretion which probably date back to their own childhood. If you are one of these people, try as hard as you can to prevent your problems from affecting your children. It is wrong to believe that your children must have at least one bowel movement in every twenty-four hours. If they have a healthy diet and don't feel anxious about excretion, a day or two here and there without a bowel movement will not hurt them. For goodness sake, don't start giving them enemas and laxatives. Some dried fruit, or a little lactose added to milk or juice will do the trick if you are really worried. Untold damage is done by mothers who are determined their children must have a bowel movement at least once, and sometimes twice a day, and who bring out the enema at the first sign of an omission.

You can encourage your children to miss the potty stage and use a lavatory right away if you put a small stool in front of it for them to climb on, and put a special seat made for children over the ordinary seat. Often, they prefer this to a potty because it seems more grown-up.

Your child will learn to use the lavatory by watching you.

Summary

1. Children do not need to be "trained" to use a potty. They learn by watching others.
2. Try not to let your "hang-ups" regarding excretory processes affect your children.

9

Bed Time and Sleep

Adults go to bed at any time they choose. If they have too many late nights in a row, they catch up with a couple of early ones, or sleep late. What happens if we treat children in the same way as adults in this area, and let them decide on their own bedtimes, too?

Up to about eighteen months, most children accept going to bed quite happily, if it is part of a cheerful daily routine accompanied by a cuddle and perhaps a story. After that age, sooner or later they begin to develop their own ideas about what time they should go to bed. There are few parents who have not had their share of bedtime battles.

As soon as my first daughter, Justine, showed signs of exerting her will over her bedtime, I let her do so. In other words, I let her decide for herself when she would go to bed. This worked very well. Most days she would become tired around 8:00 in the evening. Then she would go to bed quite cheerfully with a story and a cuddle. Sometimes she would fall asleep in the den and be carried to bed; on other occasions she would simply say she was tired and trot off to bed on her own. If we went out or had visitors, she might stay up late and sleep longer the next morning or afternoon. She was allowed to remain in the den as long as she played very quietly and did not disturb us. If there was any whining or a tantrum, or if she wanted to play noisy games when we felt like quiet, she was sent away with an explanation that we wished to sit in peace. She was not ordered to her room, but simply told that, in the evenings, we like quiet in the den, so if she wanted to make a noise, she must do so elsewhere.

When Justine was two years and eight months old, she started going to nursery school, and then things didn't work out so well. She would stay up late, playing quietly, and then become exhausted at school and fight with other children towards the end of the morning. A sleep in the afternoon did not seem sufficient to carry her through the next morning. I would explain to her that if she went to bed earlier, she would feel better the next day, but she seemed unable to grasp the connection.

After considerable discussion, reading, and thought, I realized I was coming up against two problems. One was that she didn't have a well developed time concept. "Tomorrow" didn't mean much to her, and she found it difficult to relate her lack of sleep in the evening to her fatigue the following day. The second difficulty was that she felt banished and excluded if she was sent to bed. This is especially a problem with an only or older child. She said to Leon, my husband, one day "Why must I go to bed when you are all up having fun?" When we tried to force her to go to bed early, the result was heart-breaking rows and bouts of crying which were very new in our household. This reinforced our belief that coercion is never the solution to any problem.

Once again, we applied the adult test. We asked ourselves how we would feel if someone told us every night, "You must go to bed on your own now, while we stay up and enjoy ourselves, because we have a special ability to stay up later which you don't share." It didn't sound like too much fun.

The Family Bed

At this time, I came across *The Family Bed* by Tine Thevenin. This book helped me to find the solution to our bedtime problem. The book points out that ours is one of the few cultures in which children are banished to sleep alone from an early age. The author believes that isolating children at night time, besides having many other deleterious effects, leaves them with a lasting feeling of insecurity. Her arguments are supported by those of Ashley Montagu, in *Touching*. Montagu discusses in depth the great need of human beings, especially children, for skin contact. This contact is well supplied by those cultures in which various members of the family sleep together.

The Family Bed suggests that children should share their parents' bed until they want to move out. The earlier they start sleeping with their parents, the sooner they are ready to stop, but the usual age for this is around 5 or 6 years. At this time, they often like to join a sibling. The author points out that the parents can have sexual intercourse either in another room, or after the children are asleep.

If you find the idea of having your children sleep in your bed too outrageous, there are certain compromises you might reach. What I did with Justine was this. I explained to her that she wasn't much fun to be with the next day if she didn't have enough sleep. I told her she could sleep in our bed, and if she went there at 8 o'clock I would come with her and read a story. The alternative, if she insisted on staying up, was that she must play very quietly on her own, because no one was going to entertain her. I explained that, after a long day, we wanted to relax in the evenings. I also told her that if she overslept the next day, we would not wake her up and then she would miss school and have to play alone all morning.

She opted for going to bed at 8:00 because that was the more attractive alternative. If she asked me to, I would stay with her after her story until she went to sleep. I would read my own book then, and it was never long before she fell asleep. If there was something special that I wanted to watch on TV, I would tell her, and leave her alone. We always made it clear that, if we had visitors, she must stay alone and look at her books because we were entitled to spend time with our friends, just as she was with hers. The fact she was in our bed seemed to alleviate her feelings of loneliness. When we went to bed, Leon used to lift her into her sleeping bag on the floor because there wasn't room for us all. Now we have bought a giant-sized bed and Justine and our younger daughter, Camilla, share it with us.

During the holidays, Justine reverts to staying up as long as she wants. Bedtime no longer has the old evil connotations for her. After a long day, she is tired by 9 o'clock and goes to bed voluntarily.

There are many variations on this theme that fit in with different family patterns and preferences. Children in small houses and flats where rooms aren't too isolated seem happier to stay in their own rooms than those in big houses. Many children like to sleep with their siblings. Justine tells me that when her sister is old enough to move out of our room, she will go with her. I intend to put them in a double bed. I personally have very happy memories of the years of my childhood when I slept in a double bed with my sister. We spent many enjoyable hours telling stories, tickling each other's backs, and so on. Certainly, in our case, the theory of *The Family Bed*, that siblings who sleep together fight less, was true.

When your children go to bed, it is not necessary to turn off the light and insist that they sleep immediately. Babies and children who are left with a low light never take long to sleep after a tiring day. You should never turn off the light without your child's permission, anyway. Many children go several months, or even years, needing a night light. Fears of the dark are common, especially among children who sleep alone. Eventually, they will outgrow them, if they are not aggravated by enforced darkness. Keep in mind, too, that different children have different sleep needs, just as adults do.

Bedtime Rights for Parents

Remember that, just as you respect your child's freedom, so he must respect yours. Parents are entitled to relax alone in their living room, or entertain friends in the evenings. There is no reason why they should put up with endless demands and interruptions, such as requests for drinks and the like. They should make that quite clear.

Imagine you had an adult lodger staying in your house who

If you share your bed with your small children, they will be relaxed and secure.

cavorted around your den screaming and yelling all evening, or who frequently demanded that you supply him with food and drinks after he had gone to bed. It wouldn't take long before you made it very plain that you were entitled to a peaceful evening and weren't there to cater to his every whim; but remember, too, that you wouldn't banish him to his room at 7:00 and turn off his light with a firm order to sleep or else!

Once the bogey is taken out of bedtime, and especially when a child is able to read to himself, the need to assist the transition from day to night falls away. Certainly by adolescence, when a proper time concept is established, the child will have reached the point where he is entirely responsible for his own bedtime, and is able to handle it just as we do.

Summary

1. Before they start school, children can be left to choose their own bedtimes.

2. Children have greater sleep needs than we, so on school days, they may need to be encouraged to go to bed early. A "family bed" makes bedtime a happy time.

3. You are entitled to insist on peace for yourself in the evenings.

Supplementary Reading

The Family Bed by Tine Thevenin

10

Toys and Ownership

The discussion on feeding, toilet training, and sleep has been mainly concerned with your child's freedom of choice and action. Now, let us return to the first half of the basic principle which pertains to your child's respect for other people's lives and belongings. This chapter, which deals mainly with toys, concentrates on the importance of mutual respect for property.

What is Ownership?

If your child is ever to respect the possessions of others, she must first learn what it means to own something.

If you truly own something, you can do what you like with it. You may destroy it, hoard it, share it, or keep it for yourself, give it away or sell it, as you see fit. If you allow your child to own her own toys, she will experience the full implications of private ownership for herself.

Janet understands very well that if she leaves her car out in the road, it may be stolen. That is her responsibility; but she said to her five-year-old son, Andy, "Go outside and bring your bicycle in this minute. If you don't, I will give it to the little boy down the road. Maybe he'll take better care of it than you do."

Andy's father, Dick, gave Andy an electric train set for Christmas, and then played with it himself for several days. Andy didn't get a chance to play with it until Dick became bored with the set. A few weeks later, Dick found a couple of tracks lying in the front drive. He said to his son, "That train set cost me a fortune. If you're not going to look after it, I will take it back to the shop and get a refund!"

Yet, all hell is let loose if Andy knocks over a vase belonging to his Mother, or bangs into his Dad's stereo and scratches a record. Andy is given a spanking or sent to his room for the afternoon, at the very least.

How can Andy possibly learn to treat other people's property with respect when he doesn't know what it feels like to own something himself?

In order to teach Andy what property ownership entails, Janet might have said something like this to him. "Do you remember the garden chair we left outside that was stolen? If you leave your bike there, the same thing could easily happen. You get a lot of pleasure from that bike. I think you would be wise to put it away."

Andy's Dad might have given him the train set and then offered to show him how it worked. He could have said to Andy, "I bought this for you because I always wanted one as a child. You're not playing with it now: can I have a turn, please?" Later, when he saw the tracks lying outside, he might have pointed out to his son, "If you leave your tracks there, they will rust if it rains, and I might drive my car over them by mistake. I can't afford to (or won't) buy you another train set, and if you don't look after this one, Mommy and I won't feel much like buying you other good toys in the future."

Then, if Andy knocked over a vase or scratched a record, his parents could say to him, "You know, I felt the same way about that as you do about your trike (or another prized possession). I am sure you wouldn't like it if I broke that." There are ways in which Andy might compensate for the damage he has done, which will be dealt with in the chapter on *Division of Labor.*

Sharing

When Rick came around to play, he saw Andy's trike, and immediately jumped on it and rode off. Andy yelled indignantly, "Mommy, that's mine. Rick can't have it!"

Janet: You mustn't be selfish, darling. Rick is your guest. If he wants your trike, he must have it. I won't ask friends around to play if you can't learn to share nicely.

Andy: But it's mine, it's mine!

Janet: If you will not learn to play nicely, you must go to your room.

Imagine treating an adult this way. Imagine, for example, that I come to visit you and see your new car in the drive. I promptly pick up your keys and drive off in it. When I get back you say, "Hey, why didn't you ask if you could take my car?" to which I reply, "Don't be so selfish. I'm your guest. If you can't share nicely, you must go to your room."

The tussle between Andy and Rick over the bike should have been handled something like this. Rick makes a grab for the bike and Andy yells out indignantly:

Janet: Andy, I suggest that you go and tell Rick that that is your bike and he must ask permission to use it.

Andy: But I don't want him to ride it; it's mine.

Janet: If you really don't want him to ride it, tell him so; but remember, if you don't let Rick play with your things when he comes here, when you go to his house, he may not let you play with his. Also, he might not want to come here any more, if it's no fun for him.

It may occasionally be necessary for you to intervene on your child's behalf, if her property rights are being violated by someone older and stronger than she is.

For example, if Geoff, who is ten, takes Andy's bike without asking, Janet might have to say: "Geoff, that is Andy's bike. You must ask his permission to use it. Please give it back now."

Looking After Toys

Dr. Maria Montessori, who devised the Montessori Method, maintains that, if the apparatus pre-school children work with is not kept in good condition, they cannot be expected to look after it. In Montessori schools, the instructors go to great lengths to make sure that the equipment is always kept in perfect condition, and the children are expected to keep it that way, too.

Go into almost any child's room and you will find that a large box or other container holds all her toys in a great, messy, mixed up heap. Half of them are broken and the Lego, marbles, blocks, and bricks are all jumbled together. The child doesn't even notice if things are lost or broken, let alone care. There are usually lots more where they came from, anyway.

It is a worthwhile investment of your time and money to help your children to value their possessions. Start when they are very small, somewhere around one year. Either buy or make a few shelves at a height that your child can easily reach. Don't be parsimonious; you'll be surprised how quickly they fill up. Buy some plastic containers of varying sizes and label them simply, in clear lower-case letters with the name of what they are to contain. For example "beads," "blocks," "dolls," "cars," "crayons," "playdough," or whatever. Every so often, mend broken toys or broken spines of books, and so on. As soon as your child is old enough, ask her permission before you do so, and suggest that she helps you or you help her.

If you follow these suggestions, your child will get far more mileage out of her toys, simply because they are easier to locate and more attractive than they would be otherwise. She will treat them with more respect because they are in good condition. You will feel less irritated because you won't see things that cost a lot of money spoiled and wasted. The toys will have a much longer life. Your child will learn to read a few words from the labels on her boxes, and tidying up will be less of a chore.

Tidying Up

Decide whether your child's room is hers to do with as she wishes, or not. Adults have a whole house to keep in whatever state they please. Children need a room of their own, too. Mother does not coerce Father into keeping his workshop tidy, though she might try and persuade him to do so. Similarly, in most

Provide labeled boxes for your children's toys. Then it will be easy for them to look after their possessions.

families, Father does not force Mother to keep her sewing room or study or kitchen the way he thinks it should be kept. Yet, parents commonly use all kinds of threats and punishments to make their children tidy up their rooms.

Your child should be allowed to keep her room in whatever state she chooses. Only if she experiences both tidiness and the consequences of untidiness will she learn which she prefers. You can, however, give her a good example to follow, and lead her in the right direction.

You are already half way there when you have provided shelves at an accessible height, and labeled boxes. You will have to tidy up for a baby, but as soon as your child is old enough to help in the most rudimentary way, she can start to do so. Little ones love to help, especially when it is a game, and they like to imitate their parents in everything they do. You can say to your two-year-old, "I wonder if you can find the blue blocks and put them all in this box." By the time she is three, you might suggest, "Come, let's tidy up together. I'll count to ten and we can see how quickly you can put all these beads in here."

If you make tidying up a daily habit, it only takes five to ten minutes in the evening, and may be one of the few times your child gets to play with you alone.

What happens if your child says "no" when you ask if she would like to join you in tidying up? This is not likely with a young child, unless she is busy with something else, but if it happens, you can either leave the tidying till some other time, or ask her permission to do it on your own. Remember, it is you who doesn't like the mess, not she, and it is her room. You can always leave the room as it is and close the door so you don't have to see it! You can also insist that she keep the door closed until it is tidy.

Many children nowadays receive so many toys and clothes that they lose respect for their property and don't look after it at all. Their feeling is that there is always more where that comes from. If you think this has happened to your child, then don't buy her anything new for a while. If she asks for something she sees in the store, point out that, since she makes no effort to look after her toys and clothes, you don't feel like buying her any more. When her attitude changes, you can reward her with a gift of something you know she particularly wants.

A time will come when you feel that your child has had enough experience to continue alone. If you started early enough, this should happen by the time she is eight or nine. Now, she can look after her own property independently. If her possessions break, she can mend them herself or ask your help. If her room is in a terrible mess and she can't find anything, and there is no free spot left on the floor to walk, that is her problem. Alternatively, you might feel you really can't live with the shambles in her room, and that she should tidy it up as a favor to you. You can make this clear to her, and refuse her favors if she does not comply with your wishes. You might tell her that, until she tidies her room, you are not prepared to give her a lift to visit a friend, or whatever other favor she presently enjoys from you. If you have chosen to clean her room for her as a general rule, you can point out that is impossible for you to do so right now. You can relate to her in just the same way as you do to your husband, wife, mother-in-law, or any other adult living in your home.

Summary

1. Let your children really own their toys. That is how they discover what ownership entails.

2. Encourage them to value their toys by helping them to look after them and keep them tidy.

3. Apply the adult test and don't force your children to tidy up their rooms.

11

Clothes, Furnishings, and Other Destructibles

The ownership of toys is a clear-cut issue; but when it comes to the rest of your child's room and its furnishing, you may want different precepts to apply.

If you use the adult test and regard your child as a tenant in your home, it is easier to decide what rules should apply to his room.

A tenant can do what he likes in the room, apartment, or house he is renting, provided that he leaves it in the condition in which he found it. It would be unusual to demand a certain standard of tidiness, or to tell him what he must hang on his walls or how his furniture should be arranged. If you have a lodger in your house who brings his own furniture, you do not lay down guidelines as to how it should be treated. On the other hand, if he is using your furniture, you do.

Where your child's room is concerned, establish clearly in your own mind what is his property and what is yours. Decide whether the bed or cupboards are his, or on loan. The same applies to the bedding, curtains, and so on. You are likely to consider that the walls, floor, and windows, at least, are yours, and not allow him to take an axe to them. The position concerning furnishings will vary from individual to individual.

In most cases, people regard the furnishings in a child's room as the property of the parents. They expect to pass them on to siblings or relatives, or sell them when the child has grown out of them. If this is the case, the position should be made clear to the child, and he should not be allowed to damage them. If your child starts to hack up the curtains or bedspread with scissors, or to paint or draw on the cupboards and bed, let him know that he is damaging your property, and that this is not acceptable.

If he persists, point out that no one, including you, may do that to his clothes or toys. Remove the scissors, crayons, or other offending instrument, and put them to one side. Explain that they are still his, but that until he uses them properly, you will have to keep them. He can ask to have them back when he feels ready to apply them constructively.

When I was expecting my second baby, Justine's behavior regressed. She started to paint and scribble on her bed and other furniture, and spill things on the carpet. She was apparently feeling a little insecure, and needed the extra attention which her antisocial behavior attracted. I took away her paints and colored pens, and explained that she could have them back when she felt ready to make proper use of them. Leon and I tried to spend more time with her, so that she would be reassured of our love for her. About two months later, after the baby was born, she asked for her paints and pens. Since then, she has not used them destructively.

You might think it is fine for your child to draw on the walls of his room. He enjoys being surrounded by his art work, and you are happy to have the room repainted later; or you may wish to allocate only one small wall or part of a wall for this purpose. This is a good way to satisfy what seems to be a nearly universal desire to draw on walls, and to develop eye-hand coordination at the same time. Chances are, it will save the other walls in your home, too. Decide exactly what your position is, and make sure your child knows it.

There are likely to be certain pieces of furniture in your child's room which are clearly his property, especially as he grows older— possibly something he has made himself or been given as a present, perhaps a dressing table or desk. The way in which he treats that property is entirely his own business.

Clothes

The same position usually applies to clothes as to furnishings. Some clothes are given to your child as presents. They are his to do with as he wishes. Others are intended as a loan, eventually to be passed on to other children, and they should be treated with reasonable respect.

You cannot expect your child to keep his clothes in perfect condition. Obviously, they will undergo a certain amount of wear and tear in the course of everyday living, but you can prevent him from damaging them intentionally, cutting them up for a school project, for instance, and you can insist that he change after school and put on something old.

If you can afford it, it is preferable to allow your child full ownership of his clothes. That way, he will have a better chance of becoming independent and responsible. Provided they are in limited supply, your child will soon learn that if he loses them or damages them, then he has less choice of what to wear. If your child wants to wear his best clothes to school, you can point out that then they will not be special at party time, and they might get spoiled. Then, let him decide for himself.

Always let your children choose what to wear, if they are interested in doing so. This way, they will quickly learn what is suitable in different weather conditions and for various occasions. Let them choose their clothes when you buy them, too. You only need to limit the range to the amount of money you are prepared to spend. They can decide whether they prefer short or long dresses or skirts, or whatever. It is easy to influence their taste by pointing out what colors go together, and which styles you think they look nicest in. If they know they have the final say, they will probably welcome your advice; but if they are dead set on something you think is unsuitable, let them discover for themselves whether it is or is not. Remember that the pressure to conform to the standards of children their own age is usually very great from about three years on.

My sister-in-law used to say as a child, "Why must I always put on a sweater when my mother is cold?" Many parents order their children to put on something warm because they themselves feel cold. This really is not necessary. You do not tell other adults how much clothing they must wear, and neither should you do so to children. They know far better than you how they feel, and are perfectly able to decide for themselves from the time they can communicate their wishes. When Justine was three, she decided one day that she wanted to wear a summer dress and no cardigan to school in the middle of winter. I told her I was sure she would be cold, but she insisted on the thin sundress. I put a sweater in her schoolbag. Her teacher told me she shivered all day, but refused the jersey. Fortunately, she was attending a school where she was allowed to make her own decisions. That evening, she told me she had been cold at school, and the next day she reverted to her winter wardrobe. She did not repeat the experiment; however, to this day, she wears far less in winter than I would have thought necessary. Yet, she is perfectly comfortable and her body is warm to the touch. Most of us have spoiled our circulation by overdressing from babyhood on. Given a chance to decide for themselves, children will not ruin their naturally excellent circulation. If it seems to you that your child is wearing far too little, keep in mind that children are running around all the time, while adults tend to be sedentary. If your child is unwell, you can explain to him that when his body is warm it has a better chance to heal. Children who are treated with respect respond well to reason.

When children reach adolescence, many parents find it especially hard to let them choose their own clothes, and this is the time when it is absolutely essential to do so. The clothes they like may seem extraordinary to you. You may think it is outrageous for your thirteen-year-old to wear high-heeled shoes and make-up, but remember that she is running with the herd. Your teenagers are doing what their friends do, and it is a very unusual child who steps out of line. If your child does deviate from the norm, it may be because he is an independent individualist who doesn't follow the mob. On the other hand, he may be rebelling against your authority. If this is the case, you need to examine your actions, discuss the problem with him, and try to remove the cause. Questions of this nature are discussed in more detail in the chapter on adolescence.

By laying down rules and laws concerning clothing and general appearance, you breed resentment and hostility in your children. By letting them decide for themselves, you give them the feeling that they are sensible and responsible, that you recognize that, and that you trust their judgment. If you do this, they will want to earn your regard and feel worthy of it.

Summary

1. Apply the same rules to your child's room as you would to a lodger's room.

2. Decide whether the clothes your child wears and the furnishings in his room are his or yours.

3. Do not allow your child to damage your property, but let him do what he likes with his.

4. Allow your child to choose his own clothing. He will learn by experience what is the sensible thing to wear.

12

Discipline

More soul-searching is done over discipline than any other aspect of child rearing. Parents worry if their child is excessively shy, or not doing well at school, but they are far more concerned if they have discipline problems. The reason for this preoccupation with discipline is probably that it is the area which most closely affects day to day living within the family. Every day, as new conflicts arise, tempers are lost, voices raised, and tantrums and tears abound.

Most of the world's problems are caused by people who value their own freedom to do as they choose with their lives and their property, but do not respect the freedom of others to live as they see fit. The same is true of conflicts which arise between parents and children, but it requires self-discipline to respect other people's lives and possessions, and babies are not born with self-discipline. It is an attribute which has to be acquired.

It is usually assumed that discipline must be imposed on children by adults. A child behaves badly and is punished by her parents to discourage a repeat performance. Parents seldom think in terms of self-discipline when they think of children. Self-discipline is reserved for grown-ups.

There is little merit in a child being "good" because she fears punishment. If she doesn't understand the reason why she is not allowed to experiment with Mommy's make-up, or play with Daddy's tools, then, when she thinks she won't be discovered, she'll do it anyway. Because she doesn't understand why she can do some things and can't do others, she will grow up with no integrated set of values to discipline herself by.

The Undisciplined Baby

Babies are born sociable. They prefer the human face to any other object, the human voice to any other sound, and human arms to any other place. They are also born completely self-centered. They can't be any other way. All they know is their own comforts and discomforts, pleasure and pain. Our first job is to let them know that the world is a good place to be in—a place where they feel warm, full, loved, and wanted. That way, they start off with a positive attitude toward life.

Yet, it isn't long before they must begin to learn that they are not alone in their needs and wants. There are many other people around who have requirements, too. If our little ones are going to be happy, they must learn to consider the needs of others, as well as their own.

The best way to teach them that is by helping them to stand in the other person's shoes. It is always far easier to sympathize with someone else's position if you can put yourself in his place.

Often the response to unsociable behavior in a child is "well, after all, she is just a child." This is no compliment to the child. She is a person, albeit lacking experience. She is capable of thought, of controlling her actions, and is hungry for knowledge. Her appetite for learning is insatiable.

Property Rights

Parents become very angry when their children damage their possessions. This is a major source of dispute in every household.

In order to prevent your children from harming your belongings, you need to establish exactly what property belongs to whom in your home. As discussed in Chapter 11 (pp. 71–76), a working example would be to decide that your child's room, toys, and clothes are his property. The rest of the house and its contents belong to you and your partner. You may decide your children should have a playroom, too.

Now it is up to your children to elect what they will allow others to do in their rooms and with their property. It is up to you to decide what you will allow regarding yours. You must be completely clear about it because consistency is of the utmost importance, and everyone is different. I have a friend who really doesn't mind what her children do, provided they don't break her things. Even that isn't too important. She doesn't care if they spill drinks on the floor, or mash banana into her living room carpet, or tramp mud into the house. She truly does not mind; but she explains to her children that other people don't like it, and that they must respect the property of others. I have another friend who is a stickler for cleanliness. She has a beautiful white den

suite, her house is always sparkling, and she has taught her children that they must take their shoes off before they come into the house, they must eat food only at the table, and they must not climb on the furniture.

Decide what you require. You are entitled to—it is your property. Stick to your decision unless you change your mind. If you do change your mind, then communicate that change clearly to your children and give your reason.

In Chapter 10, mutual respect for property was discussed in some detail. If your children know that their things belong to them completely, and no one is going to take them away, or even touch them without their permission, then they will understand why they should show others the same respect.

In addition to respecting their possessions, whenever your children do not respect yours, be absolutely consistent in stopping them.

Consider the following typical scene. Kevin's mother is having tea with a friend. Kevin climbs up on the couch with his shoes on and starts kicking the cushions. Five or six times, with increasing irritation, his mother says to him "Don't do that, darling." Finally, she loses her temper and pushes him roughly away from the cushions. He immediately emits ear-piercing shrieks and wails. His mother grabs a cookie and gives it to him, whereupon he subsides.

The episode should have been handled something like this. Kevin climbs on the couch and starts kicking the cushions. His mother says, "Darling, if you want to climb on the couch you must take your shoes off because you are making my cushions dirty. Kevin ignores her. His mother then says, "If you go on dirtying my things, I will have to take you off the couch." He continues. She firmly but gently picks him up and puts him on the ground. Shrieks and wails issue forth. His mother says, "Please stop making that noise. You may not make that noise in my room." Kevin continues to screech. His mother picks him up and carries him to a place sufficiently distant so that the noise is tolerable.

She says to him, "You may come back when you are quiet," and then she leaves him. She does not go back to him as long as he is throwing his tantrum.

You will notice that in the second scene, Kevin's mother has explained why she finds his actions unacceptable, and has offered him an alternative. She has immediately made it clear that she means what she says. She has not rewarded the ensuing tantrum with the attention it sought.

When my friends and I have used this approach, the results have always been favorable. I have consistently handled my children this way. I have not needed to physically remove Justine from anywhere since she was four years old. She knows that I mean what I say, and she complies with my requests. If she argues, I remind her that I respect her property. Once in every couple of months, she shouts at me, and I have to ask her to leave my room until she can talk pleasantly. She goes away, and returns within five minutes to half an hour with a big smile saying, "Sorry, Mommy," or "I'm not cross any more," or something to that effect.

Distraction

There are several good reasons for offering a child an alternative when she does something unacceptable. First of all, it distracts her. Secondly, she can take up the alternative without feeling she has given in or lost a battle of wills. Thirdly, there is a good chance she was just bored in the first place. In our example, Kevin's mother suggests that he climb on the couch barefoot. She might have offered any number of other alternatives—for instance that he take crumbs to feed the birds, or have a teaparty with his teddy bears, or whatever. Distraction works particularly well with very young children, whose behavior can easily be guided along more acceptable channels without any explanations or arguments being necessary.

Don't Reward Bad Behavior

Never reward tantrums and angry crying. Many parents will

do anything to stop their children crying and whining, including giving them what they want or diverting them with something attractive to eat. All this does is teach the child that if he makes enough noise, he will get his own way. The only acceptable reason for crying is physical or emotional pain. If your child is not getting his own way, he is not suffering emotional pain. He is angry because he is being flouted. If children are to be happy, they have to learn that they cannot always have what they want, especially if it belongs to someone else.

Whining is never desirable; however, you must give your children a chance to speak to you. Often, they whine because no one listens to them when they speak in a normal voice. They find that if they repeat themselves often enough in an objectionable tone, someone notices. You need not interrupt your conversation and jump to attention every time your child speaks. If you are talking to someone else, just say, "Wait a minute," and at the first reasonable break, turn your full attention to him and ask what he wants. If he whines, say, "I don't feel like doing anything for you when you speak to me like that. If you wait a while and then ask nicely, I will try to help you." Stick to your word.

If your child throws a temper tantrum, ask him to stop. If he will not, then ask him to go somewhere else. If he does not do that either, pick him up and carry him elsewhere. It won't take long before he learns that tantrums are unrewarding and not worth the effort.

Does He Need Attention?

Often, when children behave badly, they do so because they need attention. Sometimes, the only attention they ever get is in the form of a reprimand or a smack. Their feeling is that even that is better than nothing. If your child is persistently antisocial, ask yourself whether it isn't simply attention that he seeks. If the answer is yes, then make sure he doesn't get it when he is being unpleasant, but that he gets plenty at other times. Set aside a period of every day especially for him when you play with him, read to him, talk to him, or do anything else he wants. At other times, even if you are busy cooking, sewing, or driving, listen attentively, and respond when he speaks to you. He needs and deserves your interest and company, and should get it when he is behaving positively.

Good Manners

Just as you should not accede to whining, so you should not accept bad manners. Adults do not throw orders around left, right, and center, and expect everyone to obey (or if they do, they become very unpopular); neither should children. Explain that people don't like doing things for others unless they are asked nicely, and thanked afterwards. They especially do not want to help people who whine and holler. If your child does not say "please" when she asks for something, don't comply with her request. Explain why. Say "If you come back and ask me nicely in a little while, I might help you." If she is very little, only two years or less, you can let her have a second try right away. You can insist on "pleases" right from the time your children start to talk. Remember that children are great imitators, so always set a good example for them. In other words, never omit the "pleases" and "thank yous" yourself. If for some reason your child stubbornly refuses to ask for things nicely, she won't continue her antisocial behavior for long, provided you are consistent in not giving in to her demands. She will soon discover that getting what she wants by being polite is more fun than being ignored.

Obstinacy

People often say to me, "Oh, it's all very well for you, your children are reasonable and compliant by nature. Mine are so obstinate." Recently, a conversation that took place between a friend and me went something like this:

Friend: I have such trouble getting Grant out of the bath at night; I'm at my wit's end.

Me: Why don't you let him stay there?

Friend:(shocked) I can't do that, he would keep us all waiting for
        supper!
Me: Try starting supper without him.
Friend:Oh no, if he wants to eat, then he must eat with the family.
Me: Perhaps you could explain to him that if he doesn't get out
        of the bath when you ask him to, you will start supper
        without him; and since you do not intend providing two
        suppers, he will have to go to bed hungry.
Friend:That wouldn't work. He'd just stay in the bath all night.
Me: That doesn't seem likely. Sooner or later he would be sure
        to get bored and tired and want to go to bed, especially
        when the water gets cold. Then, maybe when he realized he
        had missed his supper and story, and had to go to bed on his
        own, he wouldn't do it again.
Friend:Oh, you don't know Grant. He is so stubborn.

Well, I think I do know Grant. Grant is interested in what makes
him happy, as are all people, but he doesn't like following an
endless series of instructions and orders. He wants to feel that he
controls his life. Given the chance to decide for himself, his
obstinacy would fall away. Resistance only arises when there is
something to resist.

The Reactor Factor

Sometimes it may seem as if your child is resisting when there
is nothing to resist. If this happens, it is usually due to a misun-
derstanding. If you take a second look at your child's reaction,
you might find that you have said something colloquial which
sounds perfectly reasonable to you, but might sound unreasonable
to someone who is not familiar with the expression.

For example, Leon once went into the Post Office with Justine
when she was two-and-a-half years old. She was sitting on the
counter while he attended to his business, and when he had
finished he said, "Come on, let's go," lifted her off the counter,
and set her on her feet. She promptly started yelling, "No, no."
Leon was completely bewildered by her violent and unreasonable

reaction; however, when we discussed the incident, we realized that, had he said to me, "Come on, let's go," I would have understood that that was not an order, but a suggestion to which he expected a positive response. To Justine, who was not aware of the assumed implications, it was an order. To her, it seemed as if he was saying "Come on, we are going now, whether you like it or not." After that, when we were leaving one place to go to another, we said to her, "I am going now, do you want to come, too?" Such a question never met with any resistance.

Cheekiness

Cheekiness is a concept which only arises between superiors and inferiors. Think about it. Imagine an adult you might consider cheeky in her behavior; it is sure to be someone you think of as inferior to yourself. Presumably, you would not call your husband, best friend, or boss cheeky, no matter what they did.

It is to be hoped that you do not consider your children your inferiors. If you do, you may be sure that they know it and don't like it. That is why they are cheeky. It is their silly way of saying, "I have rights, too, so there!" If you treat your children as equals in all but experience and knowledge, they will not be rude to you.

Often, a child does not mean anything at all by an action which may seem ill-mannered to you. He is just trying out a new trick he has seen elsewhere. Your child may stick his tongue out at you, or use an obnoxious swear word, or spit at you. Remember that he does not have much experience, and has not yet discovered what the implications of these actions are. He has simply seen someone else do something, possibly with interesting results, and he is testing its effectiveness. If you really feel strongly about his action, explain that it is not considered polite behavior. Better still, pass it off with as little fuss as possible. That is the best way to render the action uninteresting and not worth repeating.

Punishment

There are three commonly accepted forms of punishment: corporal punishment, shutting a child in a room, and withholding privileges.

Corporal Punishment

In our Western society, corporal punishment is considered too uncivilized to be used on adults. Yet, with children, it is the order of the day. This is an extreme example of the double standard which we apply to children. It is also the most obvious way in which parents try to discipline their children by training, as they would an animal, instead of encouraging them to discipline themselves.

Parents should try never to hit their children. If they do so in a fit of temper, they should apologize afterwards. Children are smaller and weaker than we are, and hitting them is bullying them. It is resorting to the use of brute force instead of reason. We are trying to teach our children to be reasonable. Assaulting them teaches them the opposite. When you hit your children, you show them that you have given up on reason, and that you are bigger than they are. The latter fact they already know all too well. You should tell them that, even though other people do it, hitting is frowned upon in your family.

It is possible to beat or terrify children into obedience, but it will be a fearful, resentful obedience. Your children will not respect you for it, and they will not learn anything good from it. It will breed lying and deviousness.

Recently, I heard on a news report that some adolescents in the United States had been prosecuted for parent battering. My reaction was, firstly, that you only hear of parents who are brought to trial for battering their children in the most extreme cases, yet it happens in almost every family all the time; and, secondly, that maybe those young people, when they found one day that they had grown bigger and stronger than Mom and Dad, decided to turn the tables.

Solitary Confinement

Shutting someone alone in a room from which they cannot escape is an extremely severe form of punishment reserved for criminals. Yet, parents often lock up their children, or shut them in rooms where they cannot reach the door handle. Perhaps the worst place to close them in is their own room because then it becomes a place associated with pain instead of pleasure. There are few, if any, children who do something so evil that it warrants the frightful frustration, anguish, and feeling of helplessness that results from incarceration. If your child persists in some antisocial act, by all means remove her from the scene of the crime, but do it gently, and don't lock her up! In the most extreme case, where she insists on returning repeatedly and continuing the unwanted action, shut her out of the room you are in. The object is to protect your rights, not to make her suffer.

Withholding Privileges

If you need to resort to punishing a child at all, withholding privileges is one acceptable way of doing so.

If your child persists in violating your rights, or does so deliberately and knowingly, you can tell her, for instance: "Since you poured my shampoo down the drain, and you knew that it was mine, I am not going to let you watch television tonight," (assuming the television set is yours) or "I am not going to take you with me to the store," or whatever other privilege your child enjoys. Do not say she cannot play with her new car, or you are taking back the toy you bought her. Two wrongs don't make a right.

Compensation

It is better still if there is no punishment at all, but your child rather repairs the damage she has done, or compensates you for it. Say she has spilled on the floor or scribbled on the wall. Then ask her to clean it. If she has broken something of yours, you can require compensation. Your child should have her own money from the age of about three years on (discussed in *Division of Labor*) with which she can buy things she wants or compensate you for any of your property which she has destroyed or damaged.

Apply the adult test. Say she has broken something by mistake which is of no great value. Then, just let her clean it up, and put it down to the cost of having small children who have such a lot to learn. You wouldn't expect an adult to replace something small broken by mistake. On the other hand, if it is something you value highly, then explain your distress. Say that you now wish to replace it, and that you expect her to pay for it. If it is expensive, that will be expecting too much from a small child, but she can at least empty out her piggy bank, rather like the sequestration of an adult who can't pay her debts. A teenager should pay the full amount, provided it isn't too vast. If the action is deliberately destructive, there should certainly be compensation. If the child has no money, she can work to earn it. You can take something she values as a pledge until she has paid off her debt.

Requiring compensation from a child is quite different from punishing her, and has several advantages. To start with, it dilutes the parents' anger and saves the child from feeling helpless and guilty. In addition, it prepares the child for the principles which apply in adult life.

I remember all too well my feelings of helplessness and frustration as a youngster when I broke something belonging to my mother and she was justifiably annoyed. I didn't mean to do it, and now it was too late and there was nothing I could do to make amends.

One day, my sister's little boy, Matthew, was playing a bit roughly with my daughter Camilla, and snatched her new bracelet and broke it. I said to him "Matty, I think you should buy Camilla a new bracelet; she loved that one so much." My sister intervened, "Oh, but it wasn't really his fault," but then she thought better and said to him, "Matt, do you think you should buy Milly another bracelet?" Matty was only five, and his bottom lip wobbled a bit as he thought of his hard earned money, but he said, "Yes, I do. How much is it?" It was twenty cents, quite a lot of money in his life, but he went to the shop and paid it out willingly, taking considerable satisfaction in making his cousin happy again. This way, no one was left with ill feelings.

Lying

Very young children, around the age of three, often blur the edges between fantasy and reality, making up stories to suit the moment. This kind of storytelling is quite different from the lies children tell deliberately when they fear the consequences of their actions. Deliberate lying will largely fall away if your children can compensate you when they do something wrong. You will not become so angry, and they will be less afraid.

There was a time when Justine started lying on occasion. Such blatant and transparent lies! I realized she must have become afraid of what would happen if she told the truth. I said to her, "It makes me sad when you lie. Then I don't know whether I can trust you or not. I'll make a deal with you. If you promise not to lie, I promise not to shout at you." She agreed. I abided by my promise for a few days, then I became angry and shouted at her for leaving a tap running and refusing to admit she had turned it on. The following morning as I walked down the corridor past the bathroom, she ran out of her bedroom, and the following conversation ensued:

Justine:Mommy, I left the tap running again because I couldn't turn
       it off.
Me: Remember what I told you darling, if you can't turn the tap
       off, ask Daddy or me to help you.
Justine:OK, Mommy, but remember you promised not to be cross
       with me?
Me: Well, I'm not cross now, am I?
Justine:No, but you were last night.

Well, I apologized and said she should tell me right away next
time I broke my promise. This is a salutary example of how your
children can discipline you!

When Force Is Justifiable

It will be evident by now that this book does not advance the
use of force in human relationships.

There are two types of situations, however, in which the use
of force is necessary. The first is in self defense. When a child
is attacking you or damaging your property and you have to
remove him physically in order to stop him, then you are acting
in self defense. This would be the same as evicting an adult from
your house if he was wreaking havoc there.

The second place where you need to use force is in defense of
other people and their property. This applies particularly to children because of their lack of experience. If a child who cannot
swim falls into a swimming pool, you have to haul him out
physically. You have to lock your gate to stop his freedom of
movement onto a busy road. You must prevent him from doing
anything to endanger himself. This is the one area where you are
justified in interfering with his freedom to do whatever he chooses.

It is no good just setting up rules and regulations, and punishing
him for not obeying them. For one thing, you are too late if you
smack him after he has burned himself on the stove. He has, by
then, learned the hard way not to touch the stove. For another,
if a child thinks the only reason he shouldn't do something is that
he might be punished if he does, he tends to become obstinate

and do it just to prove he has a mind of his own. All he knows is that, for no apparent reason, some of his actions earn smacks and others do not.

As soon as he is old enough, explain the danger involved in certain actions. Where possible, get the message home with impact. If you see a dead dog or cat lying next to the road you can say, "See that cat. He ran on the road and a car knocked him over. Now he san never run around and play again. He is gone forever and ever. That might happen to you if you go onto the road."

Until you are sure that your child understands the danger clearly, make sure that he can't get hurt. Don't make a big thing out of it; simply see that poisons are out of reach, electric plugs covered, and so on.

However, you need not be unduly concerned over your children's safety. Even in this area, they can be allowed considerable freedom because, from a very early age, they are surprisingly good at taking care of themselves, if they are given a chance.

Jean Liedloff describes in *The Continuum Concept* the remarkable success with which Yequana babies look after themselves in what we would regard as very dangerous surroundings. She tells of how she watched a baby, too young to walk, crawling and playing on the perimeter of a five foot deep pit. Occupied with a stock or some stones, he would tumble about, landing with his back to the danger, but never fall over the edge.

Small children and toddlers would play on the bank of a rapidly running river, or toy with the razor-sharp knives and matches which were lying around, or with fire brands picked up from the edge of the fire, but at no time did she see or hear of a baby falling into the pit or river, cutting himself or his mother with a knife, or setting fire to the thatch roof of a house. Their elders simply took it for granted that the children were well able to look after themselves.

Ms. Liedloff observes: a baby has no suicidal inclination, and a full set of survival mechanisms, from the senses, on the grossest

Don't be afraid to let your toddler use a blunt knife. Only experience with potentially dangerous instruments will teach her to use them properly.

level, to what looks like very serviceable everyday telepathy on the less accountable levels. He behaves like any little animal which cannot call upon experience to serve its judgment; he simply does the safe thing, unaware of making a choice.

The author assumes that if we place the responsibility on people to look after themselves, they will do so very well, but if we set ourselves up as their caretakers "...the result is diminished efficiency because no one can be as constantly or as thoroughly alert to anyone's circumstances as he is to his own."

Experiments have been done with babies in our culture which demonstrate their self-preservation instinct. In one such experiment, babies at the crawling stage were placed on a sheet of glass which partly covered a solid surface and was partly extended over nothing at all, as it was continued over the edge of a steep drop. The babies only crawled as far as there appeared to be solid ground beneath them. None of them went over the edge of the apparent drop.

Let it be clear that I am not advocating that you expose your child to every kind of danger, regardless of your better judgment. The Yequana live in a very different culture from ours. They do not have any of the "man-made" dangers in our society of which a baby can have no instinctive knowledge, such as electric plugs and swimming pools. The still, reflective surface of a swimming pool is quite different from that of a river such as Jean Liedloff describes.

What I am saying is, try not to be over-protective. Your baby won't become ill from putting dirty objects in his mouth. On the contrary, it will build up his resistance to germs; but obviously you should not let him ingest animal feces. If he is sitting firmly, playing with a blunt knife, he is unlikely to harm himself. On the other hand, if he is staggering around with a razor blade in his hand, you would do well to intervene!

Teach your child how to carry scissors with the sharp end pointing away from him. Show him how to light a match, hold it, and blow it out without hurting himself. Rather than making dangerous objects forbidden fruit, let your child learn to handle them correctly as young as possible, thus rendering them harmless.

Other People's Property

Many people feel that they should not interfere with other people's children. Because of this, you may find it necessary to protect someone's property from your children. When your little boy starts to grind his sticky candy into your neighbor's carpet, if she doesn't show signs of stopping him herself, then it is up to you to do so, removing the candy if necessary.

All of these situations where you occasionally need to use force on children apply to adults, too. When you find someone trying to commit suicide, it is usual to try and save them. You do not grant them the freedom to take their own life. You believe that, given a second chance, they might think better of their original decision.

Similarly, if a person from a primitive culture was in your home and went to investigate an electrical plug socket with a couple of pieces of wire, you would stop him first and explain why afterwards.

By the same token, if you saw a little old woman set upon by a lout who was stealing her handbag, you would probably do something to help her, despite the fact that you would be interfering in her life. The use of force is justified in these cases because it is used to protect rights.

Look to Yourself

When your child does something wrong, remember that her action, that is the tantrum, destructiveness, or lying, is a symptom of a deeper problem. Deal with the symptom immediately by withholding privileges, demanding compensation, or whatever you decide is best, and then look for the cause.

Your children are not innately bad. Everything they ever do wrong is in response to some occurrence in their environment.

When your child behaves badly, the first place to look for the cause is in your own actions. You are the most important influence in your child's life, and therefore you are most likely to be the cause of her bad behavior.

Maybe you are not respecting your child's property or independence, or you are becoming too angry over small mishaps and causing her to seek refuge in lies, or you are not paying her enough attention. There are many things you might be doing wrong. You should monitor your actions all the time.

The second place to look is among other people in her environment; her friends, siblings, schoolteachers, or whomever else she relates to regularly. The problem may lie there.

As soon as you find the cause of your child's naughtiness, you can set about eradicating it.

In the two years Jean Liedloff spent with the Yequana, she observed that aggressiveness and destructiveness were completely foreign to their children. They did not ever whine, throw tantrums, fight, or damage things. You will see from the following quote that the principles which underly their rearing are precisely those which this book advocates:

"Deciding what another person should do, no matter what his age, is outside the Yequana vocabulary of behaviors. There is great interest in what everyone does, but no impulse to influence—let alone coerce anyone. A child's will is his motive force. There is no slavery—for how else can one describe imposing one's will on another and coercion by threat or punishment? The Yequana do not feel that a child's inferior physical strength and dependence upon them imply that they should treat him or her with less respect than an adult."

Thus, although the children are given no orders at all regarding, for example, how they should play, when they should sleep, or how much they should eat; they are expected to participate in daily chores like chopping wood, fetching water, or helping with the babies on the grounds that they are naturally social and hence want to join in the work of the people.

Saying Sorry

We all make mistakes. If you do your child an injustice—if you break your word, or are unnecessarily angry, or violate his property rights—just tell him you are sorry. You will be surprised how readily he returns the same courtesy to you.

If you have been unfair, tell your child frankly that you were in the wrong, and ask her forgiveness.

Stages

Frequently, when one mother complains to another that her child's behavior is particularly trying at present, her friend will comfort her by saying, "Never mind, he'll grow out of it soon; it's just a stage."

Despite the obvious dangers inherent in this kind of generalization, it often contains a lot of truth.

That the development and maturation of humans is characterized by stages is well documented. These stages are marked by certain typical physical, emotional, and intellectual behavior patterns.

The principles on which this book is based apply, regardless of the stage of development of your child, but that is not to say that his behavior will be consistent. He might, for example, have periods when he is more fiercely independent, or introverted, or sociable than he is at other times.

The First Five Years of Life by Arnold Gesell, and *The Child from Five to Ten* by Gesell, Ilg, and Ames, are very useful reference books for parents. They describe the typical behavior of children as they grow and mature in our culture. It is both entertaining, and at times comforting, to read up on your child's age group and discover how very typical he is.

Summary

1. If we help our children to learn self-discipline, it will benefit them throughout life.
2. Do not allow your children to damage your property unless you don't mind if they do.
3. Never reward bad behavior or respond to bad manners.
4. Obstinacy is a reaction to authoritarianism.
5. Never hit your child or shut him in a room. Such actions are extremely damaging to your relationship with him.
6. If your child behaves badly, withhold privileges or require compensation.
7. Force is justifiable if it is used to stop your child from:
   (a.) damaging you or your property,
   (b.) damaging someone else or their property,
   (c.) hurting himself.
8. Do not be unduly fearful for your child's safety. Children are better at looking after themselves than is generally believed.
9. When your child behaves badly, look to yourself for the cause.
10. Say you're sorry when you are in the wrong.
11. The principles on which this book is based should be applied, regardless of what stage of development your child has reached.

Supplementary reading

Surviving With Kids by Wayne R. Bartz, Ph.D. and Richard A. Rasor, Ed.D.

13

Division of Labor

The running of every household requires a great deal of work. Shopping must be done, food prepared, clothes and dishes washed, and a certain level of cleanliness and tidiness maintained.

Most people are not thinking in terms of producing a labor-saving device when they decide to have a baby. Small babies and toddlers are, in fact, quite the opposite. They are a full-time job; but usually, a time comes in a child's life when his parents decide he should start to do some of the work he creates himself. Now commences the running battle in which many parents try to force their children, by fair means or foul, to work in the home.

In almost all families, children eventually have to leave the nest and fend for themselves. Doing everything for your children is a disservice, not a favor. The more prepared they are and the more able to look after themselves when they do leave home, the easier the transition will be. This is a good enough reason in itself for persuading children to help with the work in the house, but if you are granting them the freedom to do as they wish, how do you go about it?

All the members of a household entail a certain amount of work. Food must be prepared for them, their dirty dishes need to be washed, their clothes have to be kept clean, and they make a certain amount of mess which must be tidied up. A husband and wife come to some kind of compromise between themselves as to the division of labor in their marriage. Perhaps they both work outside the house and split the housework fifty-fifty. Often, one of them works and finances the household while the other does the housework in exchange. You need to come to a similar arrangement with your children.

The problem does not arise with a baby. They quite simply cannot do anything for themselves. Their very existence is dependent on the work of others, and most parents accept that work cheerfully in return for seeing their babies grow healthily and happily.

Make Hay While the Sun Shines

Small children, from about 18 months on, love to help their mothers around the house. Unfortunately, most mothers regard this as a nuisance, and discourage them. This is because, initially, they are more of a hindrance than a help. Nevertheless, it is worth investing a little time and energy in teaching skills and establishing good habits while your child still thoroughly enjoys them.

You can buy small brooms, dust pans, and mops, and show your child how to use them properly. He can sweep, dust, and mop alongside of you. He can learn to polish his own shoes, fold the ironing, carry plates to the kitchen, or whatever other task he enjoys and is capable of doing. *Teaching Montessori in the Home* by Elizabeth G. Hainstock, gives ideas on the best way to teach him how to do these jobs. Montessori schools for children from the age of two and a half to seven years have "home activities" in which children learn to clean windows, polish silver, wash clothes and dishes, and even to iron. Children of both sexes love to do those things.

Doing Their Own Work

From the beginning, encourage your children to do as much of their own work as they can. They can clean up any mess they make in communal areas of the house, take their own plates to the kitchen, make their snacks, pour their drinks, and tidy up their rooms. The amount that they are able to do depends very much on their age, but they should never be underestimated.

If your children leave a trail of belongings through the house and don't bother to put them away, don't enter into a battle of wills with them. Explain that they are cluttering your area of the house, and ask them to tidy up. Children who are given a lot of freedom usually do this cheerfully enough because they are not rebellious. If they do not comply with your requests, follow Shirley Conran's suggestion in *Superwoman*. Get a big box or container of some kind. Put everything into it that anyone, including adults, leaves lying around. Your children and partner will soon find it easier to clean up than to go rummaging through a box when they want something.

The question of children keeping their own rooms tidy has been dealt with in the chapter on toys. If they refuse to clear away their dirty plates, or clean up their mess in the kitchen, or let out the bath water; in other words, when the untidiness is such that you cannot dump it in a big box, you can withhold favors in the manner discussed in the chapter on discipline.

By the time your children reach adolescence, they are capable of doing everything for themselves, including washing and ironing their own clothes and preparing their own food; however, in a household, or any other place of work, for that matter, it is much more efficient to have a division of labor in which different people concentrate their energies on different tasks. Once your child has passed the age of about seven years, you can say to him, "I will wash and iron your clothes for you if you will wash the dishes twice a week," or load the dishwasher, or whatever other exchange you think is fair. If they do not want to fulfill their side of the bargain, that is fine; you don't fulfill yours. The pressure to conform to the standards of their peers is usually quite sufficient to keep children reasonably clean. If, however, your child doesn't care whether his clothes are clean or not, but you do, then recognize the problem is yours. You are washing his clothes because it makes you happy. Then do it for that reason. If he doesn't wish to attend family meals and prefers to prepare food for himself separately, then let him do that, provided he leaves the kitchen the way he found it.

Work for You

A different situation arises when you want your children to work for you, as opposed to working for themselves. Over and above the quid pro quo of "if you'll scratch my back, I'll scratch yours" are the times when you would like your children to do tasks for you simply to lessen your own work load and give you more free time to do other things you prefer. This starts early on, when you ask your three-year-old to take a message to Daddy out in the garage, or answer the phone, or turn on the TV because you are submerged under a heap of sewing. It continues when he is older and you would like him to weed the lawn or clean your car, or any other task which is rightly yours, but which you do not feel like doing.

The Basis of Human Action

Every time a human being acts volitionally, he exchanges a situation he has for one he prefers.

When you brush your teeth, it is because you prefer a clean mouth to a dirty one. When you give money to a beggar, it is because you prefer the feeling of helping him to the one of not. When you buy a bottle of milk at the store, you prefer the milk to your money, and the shopkeeper prefers the money to the milk. When you ask your child to take out the garbage in exchange for clean clothes, he does it because he prefers the clean clothes to anything he might rather do than taking out the garbage, and you do it because you prefer running the washing machine to taking out the garbage. But what happens when you want someone to do something for you, but you are not offering a service in exchange? There are four courses of action to choose from.

You can hope they'll do it out of good will, which is often the case. That means that your pleasure is their reward. You can force them to do it. You can pay them money to do it, or you can do it yourself. Let us apply the adult test to this situation. If I ask my mother to make a dress for my daughter, she may say, "With pleasure darling; I have nothing else to do and I saw a pattern the other day which I'm dying to try out," in which case I am delighted. On the other hand, she may say, "I'm really snowed under these days and I'm not in the mood for sewing. I just do not have the time or inclination to help you." I can then say, "OK, if you don't do as I ask, I am going to beat you up." Since she is an adult and can protect herself or call the police, I won't get very far that way. The other alternative is to offer her money to make it worth her while. Finally, I can do the job myself. So what I am suggesting is that, if you have a task you want your child to do for you and he doesn't feel like it, the best alternative open to you is to pay him to do it.

Money

The idea of paying children for work is frequently met with shock and horror. "I want my children to be generous and unselfish"; "You're saying that I must teach my children that they only do something if they're paid"; "I don't want to rear little mercenaries"; "The world is materialistic enough already." These are the kinds of comments I hear if I suggest that parents pay their children.

If you want your children to be generous and considerate, the best way to teach them is by example. You can make the point over small things. If you ask your son to run to the kitchen and fetch you a spoon and he refuses, you can say to him "You know, when you won't do something for me, I don't much feel like doing things for you." Next time he asks you for a favor, for example to take him to a friend's house, you can remind him of the time he didn't help you, and if you feel it is necessary, refuse the favor. If he runs errands for you out of fear of being hit or punished in some other way, or to avoid being nagged and lectured, he is not learning generosity. He is learning to be resentful, sulky, and hostile.

I hope that I have made it clear that I do not advocate that you pay your child for every job he does. I only suggest paying him for those tasks which are specifically for you and which he does not want to do out of generosity.

As for the fear of children becoming materialistic and mercenary, this idea results from the many superstitions and misconceptions which surround the concept of money. Money is a dirty word in our culture. It is called "filthy lucre," "the root of all evil," and the accumulation of wealth is generally associated with greed and avarice.

In order to clear up these misconceptions, it is necessary to digress briefly and discuss just what money is.

The History of Money

In some cultures today, and in many in the past, there was a system of subsistence living. Each family, tribe, or individual relied entirely on their own production to meet their needs. They hunted, made their own clothes, and grew their own vegetables. Over the centuries, they discovered that it was more efficient to divide labor. It saved time for one person to keep chickens and provide eggs, another person to tan hides, another to make shoes, and so on. They would then trade goods and services with one another. Very quickly, as this system streamlined production, barter and direct trade became a difficult and increasingly complex way of doing things. For one thing, different people had different needs and preferences. Perhaps Mrs. A kept a couple of cows and provided milk for the village; she needed shoes, but Mr. B, who made shoes, didn't drink milk; and Mrs. C wanted milk, but she washed clothes and Mrs. A preferred to wash her own.

Soon, people discovered that there were certain commodities almost everyone valued. These varied greatly from one place to another. They were pretty shells or beads, tea, wheat, sugar, salt and, at one time or another, almost anything else you can think of that might be generally in demand. Everyone began to build up a supply of these valued commodities so that they would have something to barter with. This was the first money. One of the most popular forms of early money was gold. Gold has many properties which make it widely acceptable, some of which are that it is easy to break into small pieces, non-corrosive, scarce, malleable, and highly valued. When someone wanted to trade, they would take their piece of gold into a shop and bite or cut off some and weigh it to find the correct amount.

It is easy to understand that lugging around fairly large quantities of gold or shells or whatever was both unwieldy and hazardous. Goldsmiths hit on the idea of opening and policing a warehouse where people could leave their assets in safety. The warehouse owner would issue a receipt saying, "I promise to pay the bearer of this receipt one ounce of gold." That was the first paper money.

Thus, all money is is a medium of exchange. It is a way in which to facilitate the exchange of goods and services. No one wants money; they want the things it can buy. It has the huge advantage of increasing your options so that millions of goods and services become available to you in exchange for your work.

My husband, who is an economist, likes to tell people when he gives speeches that he married me because he was pleased to meet a woman who liked money. No sooner were we married, he says, than he discovered that I don't like money at all. As fast as he earns it, I spend it. The point he is trying to make is that money, per se, has no value. By the same token, money has no evil qualities. It is inanimate. People can be evil, but not money. When you offer to pay your child in exchange for work he does for you, it is no different from employing a domestic servant. You have no particular object which your employee wants in return for his services, so you pay him with money, and he can take advantage of all the goods and services available to him elsewhere.

Pocket Money

When you give your children pocket money, you teach them that they can get something for nothing. If you make it clear that they

If you pay your child to work for you, he will learn the value of money and you will have more free time.

are getting it as a gift because they give you pleasure by just being around, that is OK, but it is a better idea to let them earn their money. If you don't want them to grow up thinking the world owes them a living and that collecting dole is a better way of surviving than working, then don't teach them to collect dole at home.

The Positive Spin-offs of Child Labor

There are many advantages in paying your children to work

for you. First of all, right in their own home, they begin to acquire a basic grasp of how our economy functions. They learn that everything has a value, and before long they begin to understand, in real terms, just what that value is.

I have been paying Justine for small jobs since she was two years old. Soon after she turned four, we went to the supermarket, and she kept herself amused asking me to buy everything she saw on the shelves. We had recently been reading a book in which the children visited the land of "Take What You Want." I said to her "This isn't the land of Take What You Want; everything here costs money which Daddy and I have to work to earn." She laughed, and the requests subsided. She knew from her own experience what working for money entailed. I also pointed out that she could save and earn enough money to buy things she especially wanted. If you pay your child and expect him to buy his own things, saving gifts mainly for birthdays and other holidays, he will quickly become a discerning consumer. He will learn there are certain things he cannot afford, and others he needs to save for. He will take pleasure in his independence, and derive a sense of self-worth from seeing that his work achieves something in real terms. He will learn to count and add far sooner than you expect.

Your children will also learn to bid the price of a task up and down, and compete with one another, thus getting an idea of how market forces work. We have friends who say to their three children, "I have this job to be done, any takers for fifty cents?" One child says, "I'll do it," then another chimes in, "I'll do it for forty-five cents," and the job is bid down to its market value. On other occasions, if too low a wage is offered for an unpleasant or unpopular task, my friends have to raise the fee or do the job themselves.

Another advantage is that, if your children earn money, they can compensate for damage they do to other people's property. If they break someone else's possession, they can replace it, with full understanding of what the damage has entailed in terms of loss. This has been discussed in detail in the chapter on discipline.

Your children will have more respect for their own and other people's property when they understand the work that has been invested in acquiring it.

It is not uncommon for siblings to set up a system along these lines spontaneously among themselves. When my sisters and I were younger, if my older sister wanted something from the store, she would offer to pay one of us younger ones to do the errand for her. This method developed, despite the fact that my parents didn't pay us for work in the way I suggest. Children catch on to the idea fast. The other day, Justine offered to pay me to fetch her a toy when she was in the bath. I had initially refused her request because I was busy with the baby.

By the time your children are teenagers, they should be able to take on substantial jobs for you and other people, and earn fairly large amounts of money to buy what they want. By then, you should be paying them the same as you would an outsider.

The advantages of this system of paying for work are illustrated clearly in the following example. An acquaintance told me the story of how her son had nagged her to buy him a skate board. She told him she wasn't at all keen because she thought skate boards were dangerous. Finally, she gave in and bought one for him, and not long after that he broke his leg while riding it. He was hospitalized and considerable expense was incurred. She told me this story to illustrate why giving your children the freedom to do as they wish is not always a good idea.

If the boy in this episode had been earning money, his mother could have approached the issue this way. She could have said "If you want a skate board, you must save up and buy it for yourself." That would take a lot of work, and if he succeeded, it would be because he really wanted the board badly. She could have discussed the dangerous aspects of skate-boarding with him. If he insisted on buying the board despite the risk, she could then have warned him that, if he had an accident, she was not prepared to pay the medical expenses involved. If something should happen, she would lend him the money for the doctor's fee if necessary, but would expect him to pay it back. With the protection of family medical insurance, this would not be impossible for him to do. She might even recommend his taking out his own insurance, or paying pro-rata to the family policy. If he did hurt himself, she should stick to her word. Children can only understand the consequences of their actions by experiencing them.

Another example of the kind of thing that happens when children have never handled money took place in the family of some relatives of mine. The parents had bought their son, David, an expensive bicycle. He was seventeen years old. One day he came back from school and announced that he had swapped the bike for a pair of roller skates not worth a tenth of its value. His parents were furious, and ordered him to return the skates and get the bike back immediately. David was outraged by their interference and refused to obey them. His parents then phoned his friend's house and demanded that the exchange be reversed, which it duly was. Later, David went back and swapped the bike for the skates again. His parents were convinced that they had a terrible discipline problem on their hands.

I am quite sure that, had David been handling money from an early age, he would never have made such a silly mistake, especially if he had contributed towards the cost of the bike or bought it for himself. If he had then still swapped it with full knowledge of the implications of his actions, his parents should have respected his decision. You will have noticed that they showed no regard for his property rights and humiliated him by going over his head. He was justifiably angry. The damage having already been done, they could have pointed out to him the relative costs of the bike and the skates, and suggested that if he really wanted to walk to school from now on, he advertize the bike in the paper and get enough money to buy ten pairs of skates. This was an intelligent boy who was treated like an idiot.

If you pay your children to work for you, you will have much more free time at your disposal; they will learn to handle money intelligently and responsibly; and most important of all, they will understand fully the implications of that all-important maxim: "There is no such thing as a free lunch."

Summary

1. Small children love to help their mothers; encourage them in this, and teach them to do it effectively.

2. Expect your child to do the work he creates as soon as he is old enough.

3. Money is not evil, it is simply a means of exchange.

4. If you want your child to work for you, offer to pay him. That way he learns how our economy works; he can compensate for damage he does; and he develops a real understanding of the value of things.

14

Sibling Rivalry—Is It Inevitable?

Sibling rivalry is another term for jealousy between brothers and sisters. This occurs when a child is afraid that her sibling is taking her parents' love away from her. Most people assume that this kind of jealousy is unavoidable. I would like to question that assumption.

The first question to ask is: is there a genuine reason for jealousy between brothers and sisters? Does the arrival of a new baby in fact mean that the other children are going to be less loved by their parents? Very often the answer is no—love is not like a cake which is diminished by every slice. On the contrary, it is unlimited. You can love any number of people any amount. Many parents love all their children to the same degree. They don't love them all the same way; they love them differently and for various reasons, but they do not love one more than another. When this is the case, then the children have no reason to be jealous.

Sometimes, parents do prefer one child to another. Then, problems certainly will arise and must be dealt with, but first we need to ask why a child is jealous when her parents love her just as much as her siblings. For some reason, she thinks they do not. She thinks that her sibling is more attractive to her mother and father than she is. She feels, to a greater or lesser degree, unloveable; in other words, she lacks self-esteem.

It is very common for a first child to be jealous of a second born. In that case, it is possible that the child already felt inadequate before the new baby arrived. It is more unusual, but still common, for a second or subsequent child to suffer from jealousy. If she does, it is for the same reason. She feels unloveable.

A child who has been reared according to the methods outlined in this book will value herself highly, and feel worthy of her parents' love and respect. She will be as independent as her age allows, and will have had a chance to prove her efficacy in coping with the world. Thus, she will be very secure and not afraid that another child is going to out-do her.

Assuming that your child has high self-esteem, you need not fear the arrival of a new baby; but there are a few points worth remembering in order to ensure that the event is completely problem free. These points are covered well in other books, so I will deal with them briefly and give reference.

The Age Gap

The most beneficial age between children is a minimum of three years. By the time your child is three years old, she has spread her base considerably. She no longer relies almost entirely on her mother for her sense of well-being. Her father has become very important in her life. If she is in a play group or nursery school, she will have friends and teachers who mean a lot to her, and if the circumstances allow it, she will also have developed a good relationship with grandparents and other relatives or family friends. All this makes it easier for a mother to cope with a new baby, simply because the demands of the older child for her time and attention have been reduced, and the child is less emotionally dependent on her than previously. She now has a chance to get the baby off to a good start so that he, too, can grow up secure in her affections.

Prepare Your Child

When your new baby is on the way, no matter what age your child is, explain well ahead of the birth (at least two months) what is happening. Relate the growth of the new baby to your

Prepare your child to accept the arrival of a new baby by looking at simple books about pregnancy, childbirth, and babies with her.

child's own life. Explain that she, too, grew in your uterus and was born in the same way, and was little and helpless in the beginning.

A book with pictures of the development of the baby *in utero* will interest any child from about two years on. You can let her feel your tummy, and if she feels the baby moving, it will be more real for her. Explain how you are going to feed, bathe, and dress the baby. You can read the Ladybird book *Talk About Babies* with her, and other books written specially to prepare children for the arrival of a sibling.

When the Baby Arrives

When the baby arrives, try not to cut back too much on the time you spend with your older child. Fathers can help greatly by stepping in to fill the gap. If the mother has been working and stops, now she will have more time than before for her older child and the problem will not arise. You do not have to fall over backwards trying to prove the baby doesn't take up time; he does! Simply explain that a baby is a lot of work, not all enjoyable work at that, and that you will have less time at your disposal for a while. You do not need to cuddle the baby only when your older child is not around, dropping him hurriedly as soon as his sister appears; that is unnatural, and you can be sure it will only arouse suspicion. You love the baby and you love your other child too, in quite different ways and for quite different reasons. That should be apparent from your actions. If you don't think it is, then put it into words. You can say something like "I have to do everything for the baby because he is so small. I'm glad that you are big and able to help me and do things for yourself." Give your child a chance to help and play with the baby. Don't jump nervously every time she touches him. She is not going to do any damage. In some cultures, four and five-year-olds look after babies single-handed. Among African tribes, five-year-olds carry babies on their backs for long distances.

Baby and Child Care (Dr. B. Spock), *Between Parent and Child* (Dr. Haim G. Ginott), and *The Womanly Art of Breast Feeding* (La Léche League manual) all deal well with any problem that may arise due to some degree of jealousy in a child who is not completely secure.

Because I had been led to believe that jealousy was inevitable, I looked forward to the birth of my second child with some trepidation, but when Camilla arrived, there was quite simply no problem with Justine at all. She was four years old. I could find no evidence of jealousy, except for a couple of insignificant actions which I am not even sure resulted from jealousy. For example, when Camilla was about two weeks old, Justine asked me to put a diaper on her. I did as she asked, with little comment other than to say something like, "So you feel like playing at being a baby do you?" She wore the diaper for about an hour on three or four occasions and then took it off. Maybe this resulted from some mild feeling of jealousy, but I have no reason to believe that she wasn't simply playing "babies" in the same way that she played "mommies," which she did far more often.

Justine always derived a great deal of pleasure from playing with Milly when she was a baby, and otherwise went about her business just as before. She enjoyed showing Milly off to friends and relatives, and the only demands she made were not for my time and attention, but the baby's! She often said to me, "It's my turn now Mommy, I want to play with my sister, now." Her sister enjoyed the games as much as she did. Their relationship was enhanced by sharing a bed. Justine was thrilled and touched when Camilla snuggled up to her in the early morning. I honestly do not believe that Justine has at any time been afraid that we love Camilla more than her. It doesn't enter her head. She can see quite well that Camilla is completely different from her and that she is loved for different reasons. Naturally, their relationship changes somewhat as they grow older, but there is never any serious animosity between them.

I have two friends who have reared their children in a similar manner who also experienced no jealousy problems, and both had a two year gap to contend with, against my four year gap. One of these friends had an added complication. Her second child developed pneumonia at two months and she had to visit him in the hospital several times a day to feed him. She also slept at the hospital while her two-year-old stayed with his Grandmother. Despite that, the two-year-old showed no signs of jealousy at all.

If You Prefer Babies

There are many women who do prefer babies to older children. This is because, once their children become mobile and begin to think for themselves, the running battle of wills commences.

When a mother is constantly trying to make her child toe the line, the result is an endless series of tantrums, rebellions, and tears. Little wonder she prefers the tiny baby who is so totally dependent on her decisions! Children are usually much more sensitive to unspoken feelings than adults; they have not yet built up the defense mechanisms that we have. There is no way you can prevent a child from knowing if you prefer your baby to her. If she senses that, she will certainly be jealous, with considerable justification.

I would suggest to any mother who prefers tiny helpless babies to older children that she ask herself why. She should examine her answers very carefully, in the light of what has been said in this book about the value of independence, individuality, and self-esteem. If, in the end, she still prefers tiny babies, then she had better try to explain to her older children that that is the case. She could say something like, "I like the baby so much because he is helpless and needs me and can't decide for himself. I felt the same way about you when you were tiny." That might be painful for a child to accept, but at least it is not as confusing as knowing her mother prefers the baby, but not understanding why, and thinking it is because she is deficient in some way.

If You Prefer One Child to Another

Not all parents love their children to the same degree. Some prefer one of their children to another for a variety of reasons.

If one of your children is more easygoing and confident than another, ask yourself why. I'm not talking now about personality traits like sociability or solitariness, but about an inner sense of well-being that every child should have. You are doing something wrong with your less well-adjusted child. Examine your actions, and you will find that, in some way, you are putting that child down. Set to work building her up, and you will have another happy, loveable child.

If, on the other hand, you prefer one of your children, not because she is intrinsically more loveable, but because she is very good looking or particularly artistic, mathematical, outgoing, or whatever other trait you, for personal reasons, especially admire, then recognize that. Your more loved child isn't a better person, she just appeals more to your personal preferences.

Next time resentment arises, explain to your less preferred child, "It is not because your sister is a better person than you that I sometimes favor her, it is because she is petite and artistic. I would have liked to have been that way myself, and that makes me particularly value that quality in her." In other words, tell the truth, whatever it may be. That may be hard for both of you, but admitting that the problem lies with *you,* and not with your child, will make it easier for her to cope.

Your Children Are Individuals

"The thing that makes each child secure in his family is the feeling that his parents love him and accept him for himself." (Dr. H. Ginott, *Between Parent and Child.*)

Each one of your children is unique, and should be treated as such. Comparisons are a breeding ground for rivalry. The way to emphasize your child's uniqueness is not by saying, "Why can't you be tidy like your brother," or "clever like your sister"; that creates resentment. Simply show your children, in various ways, that you admire their respective good qualities, and allow them to experience the logical consequences of their faults.

There is no point in making meaningless statements like, "What a good boy you are." Rather, say, "I do enjoy having you at home in the afternoon; you are such a help to me with the baby." Be specific, and if you feel you must point out a weakness, don't criticize the child, criticize the action. When your son persistently leaves his cups in the den, instead of saying, "I don't know what I did to deserve you, you are impossible to live with," say, "It makes me angry when you leave your cups in the den after I have asked you repeatedly to put them away. I am sure you wouldn't like it if I left my dirty cups in your bedroom."

Your children are not equal and should not be treated as if they are. When you buy a gift of clothing for one, you need not rush out to match it with something for the others. On one occasion, you might see a certain book which you know applies to your son's current interest in dinosaurs. You can buy it for him, and if your other children object, you can tell them, "Thomas is particularly keen on dinosaurs right now; that is why I bought him this book." At another time, the same sort of situation will arise with respect to another child.

You buy someone a gift because you want to give them pleasure, not because you are afraid they will be jealous if you don't. Apply the adult test, and imagine that you buy your mother some flowers which you know she will enjoy. Do you then immediately buy some chocolates for Dad, too, in case his nose is put out of joint?

If you encourage your children to count favors, you are encouraging them to behave like state supported welfare organizations all bickering for a share of the taxes. The assumption is that all they need to do is exist in order to deserve hand-outs.

Fighting Between Siblings

When small children fight, the reason is often not rivalry, but boredom. When your kids have been playing happily for an hour and then you hear a quarrel begin, it is frequently enough just to step in quietly with a suggestion for a new game. *What to do when "There's nothing to do"* by the Boston Children's Medical Center and Elizabeth M. Gregg is one of several books full of ideas to keep children busy.

When children are quarreling for a "good" reason, that is, something other than boredom or the desire for attention, the subject of the dispute very often concerns property rights. Perhaps Jane has taken Mary's hairbrush, or John is pestering Peter when he is trying to do his homework. Do not interfere unless you really are sure someone is being bullied who cannot stand up for herself because she is too small or weak, or unless you are invited to intervene. Then, ascertain what the problem is, and if you think your children can sort it out alone, let them do so. Say "I think you can sort this

Your children will learn to settle their own disputes if you do not interfere.

out for yourselves." If you think they need a pointer, then give it, but avoid taking sides. If Jane has taken Mary's hairbrush, do not order Jane to "Give that back!" Rather, say, "Jane, you know that is Mary's hairbrush. If you don't want Mary to take your things without asking, I suggest you don't take hers."

Property rights disputes often arise when children share a room. Similar problems arise between adults sharing a room! Your child is rightfully annoyed if her brother is refusing to help while she tidies up all the toys they have both been playing with. The easiest way around this is to divide the room in two with a screen or curtains, or simply a painted line. Give each child her own containers for her toys, clothes, books, and so on. Each can then be responsible for her own property.

A final suggestion as to how to avoid ill feelings between your children is to buy their toys and clothes from them before you pass them on. It isn't at all reasonable to expect your three-year-old to sit happily watching her new baby brother get all her old toys without her permission. Chances are that she feels possessive about her things. You can ask if she wants to give them to her brother, and if she says no, then offer to buy them. Then she can buy something else with the money, and resentment won't build up. If she refuses to sell them, that is her prerogative. In *Baby and Child Care*, Dr. B. Spock points out that "... forcing a child to share his possessions when he is insecure and selfish makes those traits stronger and more lasting." When your children get older, they can buy things from each other.

Summary

1. In families where parents do not love one child more than another, children have no reason to be jealous.
2. A child with high self-esteem will not suffer from jealousy because she will feel worthy of her parents' love.
3. Rivalry is less likely to occur if there is an age gap of more than three years between your children, and if you prepare them aduquately for the arrival of a new baby.
4. If you prefer babies to older children, or like one of your children better than another, it is best to admit it and explain why.
5. Show your children that you value their individuality.
6. Children squabble when they are bored, want attention, or their property rights are violated. They should settle their own disputes whenever possible.

15

Sex Without Guilt

The thesis of this chapter is that, if the subject of sex was treated completely openly in the family, and if children were allowed total freedom for sexual exploration and development, then sexual problems and perversions would cease to exist in our society.

Sexual activity is as important to human beings as sleep, food, and the need to control their environment. We are sexual by nature. We have physiological organs and characteristics, and hormones which have no other purpose than the reproduction of our species. Yet, even in this "emancipated" age, the whole subject is clouded and distorted by taboos. We still find it difficult to talk about sex as freely as we do about food or sleep or work. Sex is the major subject of jokes. Apparently, we only feel comfortable talking about it if we can laugh away our embarrassment.

The Origins of Taboos

How did all these sexual taboos arise? There are many different theories concerning this, but it is clear that all taboos fall into one of two main categories. They have either a rational or an irrational basis.

It seems likely, for instance, that some taboos arose around sex simply because it gives so much pleasure. When primitive men wanted to appease their gods, they sacrificed those things which they enjoyed most; good food and wine, animals, and even life itself. One of the greatest sources of human pleasure is sex, so it was a natural candidate. This idea has been carried through to the present time in many religions. Still today, priests and priestesses (nuns) of certain sects are celibate. This is an irrational reason for sexual taboos, unless we believe in an irrational God who equips us for pleasure only to see us sacrifice it.

Certain primitive tribes have rational reasons for taboos. For example, Margaret Meade, in *Sex and Temperament in Three Primitive Societies*, relates an interview with an Arapesh man concerning incest. When she asked the man if he would like to have sex with his sister, he answered to this effect: "That wouldn't do. I might enjoy it; then I would have to marry her. Then I would lose out on a whole set of relatives to hunt with, and I would also have less help in planting yams and taro roots." Here, the taboo has a functional reason which the society understands. A parallel case in our society occurs when we are told that incest might result in children being born with genetic weaknesses or defects. In the past, many taboos arose to protect girls from unwanted pregnancy. The highly developed contraceptives of the twentieth century have rendered these "double standard" taboos redundant.

The trouble is that we are very unclear about which taboos in our society have a rational basis and which do not. We are victims of our own mindless conditioning. The real tragedy is that any book you pick up on sexual problems and deviations will explain that they arise from early experiences with taboos which warp the child's basic attitude toward sex.

Unfortunately, most of the books which have good discussions on how children should be raised regarding sex are specifically concerned with sexual deviations and maladjustment or happy marriage. By the time we read them, it is too late. Books on child rearing tell you to answer questions truthfully and not to worry if your child masturbates. Otherwise, they gloss over the whole uncomfortable subject.

From all the evidence at our disposal, we can deduce that, if we want our children to grow up with a happy, healthy attitude toward sex, that is to say to enjoy sex and not be crippled by hang-ups or driven to deviation, then the way to go about it is to treat the matter as naturally as we can.

Anthony Storr tells us that guilt is a primary cause of sexual deviation, and that the child's acceptance of his developing eroticism is most strongly affected by his parents' attitude toward it. "But the attitude of society as a whole is also a potent influence in causing guilt, and this is particularly true of our own Western civilization, which is far less tolerant of sexuality than many cultures." (*Sexual Deviations*, pp. 10–11).

When Storr speaks of deviation, he is talking about sexual inferiority, sexual guilt, sado-masochism, fetishism, transvestism, female and male homosexuality, exhibitionism, frotterism, voyeurism, buggery, and paedophilia.

Let us take a look at the position regarding sexual deviation in a society with very few sexual taboos.

The Trobriand Islanders

The Trobriand Islanders of North Western Melanesia were studied intensively by Bronislaw Malinowski, and his findings are discussed in his books *Sex and Repression in Savage Society,* and *The Sexual Life of the Savage.*

Malinowski found that the Trobriands have only two sexual taboos of any significance, and those are incest taboos applying to brother and sister, and to mother and son. Apart from these, their attitude toward sex is completely relaxed and permissive.

The Trobriand babies are breast fed for two to three years, and they experience almost no severity or discipline, little training, and hardly any moral education. They sleep with their mother until they choose to leave her bed.

Because the Trobriands are not aware that conception results from sexual intercourse, they do not know that fathers are related to their children. The father regards his children as a valued gift from their mother, and he assists a great deal with their early needs. The children seldom see their parents quarrel, and hardly ever see their father brutalize or ill-treat their mother. The fathers remain always interested in their children, sometimes passionately so, and play with them often. The authority over the child is vested in the maternal uncle, so the father has to win his children's love in order to retain his influence over them. Often, a long-lasting relationship develops between the father and his children, and he is regarded as "a beloved and benevolent friend."

The children run around naked until puberty. Their excretory processes are regarded as normal, rather than disgusting, and Malinowski could find no evidence of "the subterranean world of children indulging in clandestine pastimes around excretory functions and exhibitionism" which exists in our culture.

There is no repression, censure, or moral reprobation of the infantile sexuality of a genital type that develops around five to six years of age. At this age, there is still no strict discipline or compulsory education. The children now form a juvenile community in which they obey the commands of child leaders. Parents never interfere or bind them to any routine. At the age of about six to nine years, the maternal uncle starts to give the boys some training in gardening, fishing, and carrying crops, and to teach them traditional myths and legends. As far as their father is concerned, the children cooperate with him and assist him in his work out of good will.

At this stage, the children play sex games just as they do any other game. They learn about sex from older children and friends, and by observation. The games in which they play at being husband and wife and having sexual intercourse are rich with imagination and elaborate romantic interest. Although they are expected to be reasonably discreet with their sex games, adults regard them as any other game, and never interfere or disapprove.

There are no initiation rites at puberty, but at this time, boys and girls start gradually to take on a more active part in adult work. This increases until, by the end of puberty, they are fully active members of the tribe. At puberty, the boys enter special houses which are owned by a mature youth or young widower, each having three to six young tenants. There, they are joined by their sweethearts, and form a relaxed kind of group marriage. The girls move freely from one house to another, and on rare nights of chastity, may sleep at home.

The young girl has a close relationship with her father, who is also in charge of her matrimonial arrangements. Sexual intercourse between them is not strictly tabooed, as he is not considered to be her blood relative; however, it is heavily frowned on because of his relationship with her mother. Since the young girl has plenty of sexual activity elsewhere, it seldom occurs with her father.

When a girl becomes pregnant, a man considers it an honor to marry her and receive her gift from the gods. Marriage is permanent and, except for that of the chief, monogamous.

You will observe in this brief description of life among the Trobriand Islanders that their open and free attitude toward sex is linked to a general lack of authoritarianism in the rearing of the children, just as this book advocates.

Now, let us take a look at the result of this combination regarding their general sexuality and behavior.

Malinowski remarks: "Freud has shown that there is a deep connection between the course of infantile sexuality and the occurrence of perversion in later life. On the basis of this theory, an entirely lax community like that of the Trobrianders, who do not interfere with the free development of infantile sexuality, should show the minimum of perversions. This is fully confirmed in the Trobriands'. (pp. 89–90).

Violation of a child is unknown, and the idea of an adult joining in the children's sex games is thought ridiculous and disgusting. The Trobrianders have no Oedipus complex, and Malinowski could find no signs of mental illness, no nervous tics, compulsory actions, obsessive ideas, or idiocy. There was very little violence or crime of any kind.

Homosexuality was not practiced among the Trobrianders; indeed, they found the idea ludicrous, until they were subjected to white sexual mores. This happened when the boys and girls were isolated from each other on a mission station, at which time they resorted to homosexual practices as an alternative to the heterosexual activity which they regarded as their natural right. Malinowski writes, "...there were a few cases in which 'evil doers' caught *in flagrante delicto*, were ignominiously banished from the face of God back to the villages, where one of them tried to continue it, but had to give up under the pressure of native morals, expressed in scorn and derision." (p. 90).

The inhabitants of the neighboring Amphlett island, by contrast, have a number of sexual taboos, and the author found their nervousness and belligerence remarkably different from the demeanour of the "open, gay, hearty, and accessible Trobrianders."

The Mailu, inhabitants of a portion of the South Coast of New Guinea, share with the Amphlett islanders both a strict, repressive code of sexual morals, and the various neuroses of which the Trobrianders are so strikingly free.

The only problems that the Trobriands do seem to have experienced regarding their sexuality were those which sprang from the brother-sister taboo which was imposed with great rigidity, and caused considerable incest temptation. Between mother and son, where the taboo was much less strongly imposed, incest temptation was apparently almost absent.

Repression Leads to Violence

Research done by James W. Prescott strongly reinforces the supposition that the general lack of violence amongst the Trobriands is another beneficial result of their free attitude toward sex.

Prescott's research is presented in his paper *Body Pleasure and the Origins of Violence*. Among other studies, he examined 49 cultures to discover the relationship between physical affection for infants and free adolescent sex, and violence. He found: "The results clearly indicated that those societies which gave their infants the greatest amount of physical affection were characterized by low theft, low infant physical pain, low religious activity, and negligible or absent killing, mutilating, or torturing of the enemy. These data directly confirm that the deprivation of body pleasure during infancy is significantly linked to a high rate of crime and violence..." (p. 66).

In addition, Prescott discovered that those societies which impose a repressive sexual code on their adolescents negate or reduce the positive effects of holding and cuddling their children as babies.

Conversely, if a society deprives its babies of physical contact, but is tolerant of premarital sex, the detrimental effects of early deprivation are ameliorated.

Those societies which are both tolerant of teenage sexuality and physically affectionate with their infants have only a 2% likelihood of being physically violent. "The probability of this relationship occuring by chance is 125,000 to 1."

Prescott advocates premarital sex among teenagers as both natural and desirable. He believes that parents should provide a supportive environment for their children's early sexual experiences, and that this would encourage in teenagers a mature attitude toward their sexual relationships.

Where Do We Go Wrong?

All children experience certain sexual feelings. Although the sensation is nowhere near as strong as it is after the activity of the gonads (primary sex organs) increases, friction on their sex organs feels good.

A happy, active child is far too interested in discovering all the wonders in the world to be particularly interested in masturbation, but he will play with himself from time to time, and enjoy it. Your baby gets pleasure from his diaper rubbing on him, and from being washed, powdered, and creamed.

Michael S. Wolfgang, in *Male and Female Sexual Deviations*, says: "A baby will masturbate. A child should masturbate; but a hardriding parent, bearing down the full weight of frantic wrath on his little boy or girl, can cut off this activity and at that stroke, cut off all chances of the child's developing into a happy, sexually capable man or woman."

In *The Enjoyment of Love in Marriage*, Le Mon Clark clearly illustrates the effect of treating sex differently from other matters. He points out that, if a four-year-old asks his mother for an orange, he is likely to get one without much trouble. At the worst, he might have to agree to eat his spinach for supper. "Suppose, by contrast, his mother flared up, slapped his hand as he reached for the orange, and insisted that he never speak of oranges again. Indeed—her distress makes it clear, if she does not say so—no really nice boy would even *think* of oranges! He is a naughty boy and ought to know it. Mother is upset by the whole episode and wants him to realize it." (p. 10). Then his desire, denied normal expression, would find guilt-laden secret ways to express itself.

If you see your child masturbating, there is no reason why your reaction should be any different from seeing him scratch an itch. If he masturbates in public, you might tell him that that will upset people and it is better if he only does it when he is alone. If he is old enough to understand, which he certainly is by the age of four, you can say, "A lot of funny ideas have grown up about sex, so that people may be upset if you do harmless things. It's better not to upset people and make them angry if you can avoid it."

Yet, the time to talk about sex is not only when your child discovers for himself that his sex organs give him pleasant sensations. If sex is generally a taboo subject in your household, when your child does find out about it elsewhere, he'll wonder why there is so much secrecy concerning this matter in his home. How come we talk about everything else and not "that"? If he never hears what his sex organs are for, he'll assume that they are there for excretory purposes only. The only thing he really notices is that feces and urine come from that part of his body. He has been taught not to play with his excrement and that it carries germs, so he will find the idea of intimate contact with that area of his body obnoxious. I remember all too well how disgusted I was when, at the age of twelve, friends at my ballet class told me "how babies are made." What a filthy practice, I thought. On the way home in the car, I said to my mother, "I'm never going to be married." She replied, "Oh, I expect you will change your mind one day." It is a pity she didn't ask me why I had suddenly taken an aversion to marriage because, had she known the reason, a few gross misconceptions would have been cleared up much sooner than they were.

A child forms all his basic attitudes by the time he is five. When you act as if sex doesn't exist, that affects his attitude toward it. He will get ideas about it from his friends and school, too, and you can be sure they will be all bound up with naughtiness, dirtiness, and secrecy.

Your Attitude toward Your Body

Many books on child rearing and child psychology maintain that you should not be seen naked by your children of the opposite sex, and you should not allow them into your bed with you. These books argue that, if you do, your children will be bedeviled by desires they do not understand and cannot handle. The Trobrianders are just one of many examples which give evidence to the contrary.

When we hide our bodies from our children, and exclude them from our beds, we envelop our sexuality in a cloud of secrecy. That does them more harm than good. If you feel happy and relaxed sharing a bath with your children, go ahead and do it. The effect will be either neutral or positive; it certainly will not be negative.

Your Attitude toward Sex

Assuming that you sometimes want to make love when your toddler is around, don't wait until he is asleep, or say, "Go away now, Mommy and Daddy want to be alone." You don't do that when you want to talk privately, you say, "Please leave us alone, we want to talk privately." So if you want to make love say, "Please leave us alone, we want to make love (or have sex)." A time will come when your child will ask "Why?" or "What is making love?" Then answer the question. Say "We like to do it; it feels good," or "We cuddle and kiss and caress each other, and Daddy puts his penis in my vagina."

You don't have to go the roundabout route of waiting for questions as to where babies come from. The fact is that most of us make love frequently with no intention of making a baby.

Your child should know what the penis, vagina, clitoris, testicles, and labia are. They are functioning parts of the human body. Some of them are less obvious than others, but the heart, lungs, and intestines are not obvious. That does not stop us from naming them and discussing their functions.

When questions about how babies are made do arise, if the nature of sexual intercourse is already clear, it is easy to explain the connection.

Privacy

Sooner or later, your child will want to know why he should go away when you have sex, or he will ask to watch. You can tell him, "We like to make love in private. We enjoy it more that way."

Some parents do not mind if their children are around when they have intercourse. If you do not mind, that is fine. Many children all over the world have observed adults having sex, and if they understand what is happening, you would be surprised how little it interests them.

Friends of ours went on vacation recently and had to share a room with their two boys, aged three and five. When my friends wanted to make love, they proceeded to do so. The younger boy said to his brother, "What are they doing?" The older one replied, "Mating, of course," whereupon they continued playing with their toys.

If your children learn about sex this way, they will know that it is an enjoyable activity which their parents share because they love each other. Presumably, that is what you eventually want them to know.

You need not be afraid that, because your children know that you enjoy sex, they will become obsessed with it. You do not spend all your time making love, and your hormone level is a great deal higher than theirs. Different things appeal to different age groups. I spend a lot of time absorbed in writing this book. Justine spends a few minutes now and then imitating me by working on the typewriter. That is all. She doesn't want to write a book.

The Requirements of Society
Most people in our society find the idea of children who are

knowledgeable and open about sex radical and shocking. Do not let your children find this out the hard way.

Tell them as soon as they can understand, which is as early as they can understand what sex is, that many people have very odd ideas about it. Explain that if they want to ask questions about it, they should come to you or some other person you know with similar attitudes. Make it clear that if they talk about sex freely in front of Granny, or their school teachers, or their friends' parents, those people will be shocked and upset. It is not easy to explain centuries of taboos and cultural irrationalities to a three-year-old, but you can, if you keep it simple. Your children are growing up in a society with a gigantic sex problem, and that is just one more fact of reality which they must come to terms with.

Adolescence

In *Male and Female Sexual Deviation,* Michael S. Wolfgang says: "In adolescence, the full, overwhelming force of sexual drive surges forth in the individual. At best, the situation is a shock for which no amount of preparation can be adequate. At worst, the poor teenager, already bedeviled by nameless terrors and guilts about sex and the relentless pressure of his gonads, becomes hopelessly preoccupied with sexuality. He is driven to any number of antisocial activities." (p. 18).

If you have been treating sex as a natural, positive activity, your children will reach adolescence with very few feelings of guilt about it, and you will not need to worry about them. You cannot fully prepare them for sex any more than you can fully prepare a first-time mother for childbirth, but you can be confident that they are free of the guilts and obsessions that lead to deviation or repression.

Now, they only need to learn the finer details of menstruation and contraception. You can talk a little about the responsibilities babies incur, and discuss the taboos which arose largely because of unwanted motherhood. You can help your daughter to have proper contraception, and encourage your sons to realize that it is their responsibility, too, and that they, too, will have to bear the consequences of carelessness, even though they will not be carrying the baby.

If your children have developed healthy attitudes toward sex, they are not going to rush off to bed with everyone they see, or contract venereal diseases. Much more likely, they will have good sexual experiences with a few people they like a lot.

Remember that, in many parts of the world at many times, adolescents have entered into marriage, borne children, and reared them successfully. If the thought of your thirteen-year-old making love appalls you and you feel you really cannot condone adolescent sex, consider carefully the consequences of our double standard morality and sexual taboos.

In *Male and Female Sexual Deviations,* Wolfgang eloquently describes how, unfortunately, our efforts to keep our boys "clean" and our girls "pure" results in the closing off of normal heterosexual activity which could, and which does in some societies, relieve these sexual needs." He paints a vivid picture of the intense frustration experienced by an adolescent boy when he dates a young girl who is provocatively dressed, painted, and perfumed to enhance her desirability. He may hold, kiss, and touch her, but he can never release his desire in full sexual intercourse with her. Alone at home after his date, the boy fantasizes about his girl as he masturbates to relieve himself. "But his fantasies will contain elements of pure frustration and anger, as well as elements of pure sexual content. He imagines the girl will want him so much, she will do anything to get him. He may revenge himself on her for making him ache so by first imagining he beats her, or that he will refuse her until she begs him to take her."

The young girl suffers similar torments. She is just as aroused as the boy by their encounter, and wants to give in to his pleading as much as he wishes her to. She is stopped only by her fear, and in order to continue controlling her desire, she must exaggerate her fear more and more.

She, too, turns to masturbation for relief—and maybe in her fantasies, the boy refuses to listen when she says, "No," and forces her to give in to his demands.

In this account, we can clearly see the roots of several of the common deviations known to our culture.

The Double Standard

It should not be necessary even to mention the antiquated double standard that has been applied to boys and girls regarding sex, but unfortunately it is still very prevalent in our culture.

There should be only one difference in the way you approach the subject of sex between your sons and daughters. Your daughters need to be taught to take care of their own contraception because no one else is going to take care of it for them.

Apart from that, it is generally true that, in our society, boys find it easier to enter into light, uninvolved sexual relationships than girls. This may be because girls have an instinctive desire to find a permanent mate who can provide a home for their future children. Alternatively, it may simply be a product of cultural conditioning. Either way, the sexual attitudes and behavior of your sons and daughters are an entirely personal matter.

Your daughter's sex life will be influenced by the fact that she will be pursued and find any number of boys willing to go to bed with her. She will respond to this by being selective. Your boy's sex life will be affected by the fact that he will find many girls are filled with fear and guilt. He will have to learn to cope with that.

Your daughter will find that some boys think a girl who has sex is "easy" or sluttish. She will learn to avoid those boys. Your son will find girls who think he "only wants them for one thing." He will learn to keep clear of those girls.

You can talk to your children about why people develop these attitudes, and different ways of dealing with them. You cannot experience their difficulties for them or cope for them; they have to do that for themselves.

If you have a teenager with whom you have never discussed sex, then do so, and the sooner the better. An excellent book for adolescents to read is *The Facts of Love* by Alex and Jane Comfort. This book has a relaxed, positive attitude toward teenage sexuality, and advocates a responsible and intelligent approach to sexual relationships. It debunks all the prevalent myths concerning sex, pregnancy, childbirth, and venereal diseases, and answers every question your teenager is likely to have in a frank, lively manner with which he can easily identify. If you cannot get this book, but communicate well with your teenager, try to help him clear up all his misconceptions. Then leave him alone to learn. I know this is hard, but far rather he learns now than that later he has a couple of broken marriages, and possibly never experiences a normal sex life, or even becomes severely deviant.

Fortunately, the sex drive is strong, and people are remarkably resilient and tend toward normalcy. They end up alright if they are given a chance. You can help by explaining that it is your own up-bringing and neuroses that have made it hard for you to discuss sex in the past, if this is the case.

Summary

1. If you want your children to have healthy, happy sex lives when they grow up, you should treat the subject of sex as naturally as possible.

2. Societies with few sexual taboos and free adolescent sex have no sexual deviations.

3. You should tell your children about sex from an early age, in the same way as you tell them about any other important aspect of their lives.

4. Explain to your children that other people have strange ideas about sex, so they must be careful what they say.

5. Teenage boys and girls should be free to experiment sexually if they want to.

Supplementary Reading
The Facts of Love by Alex and Jane Comfort

16

Education and Miseducation

"A child has a built-in drive to explore, to investigate, to try, to seek excitement and novelty, to learn by using every one of his senses, to satisfy his boundless curiosity; and this drive is just as innate as hunger, thirst, the avoidance of pain, and other drives previously identified by psychologists as 'primary' . . . (Joan Beck: *How to Raise a Brighter child*, pp. 48–49).

Institutionalized compulsory State schooling does what it can to kill this drive. It teaches children that their interests are unimportant, that they don't know what is good for them, that the authorities have all the answers, and that, if they don't follow the dictates of those authorities, there is no hope for their future.

Fortunately, you are not forced to send your child to school before she is six years old, and by then she has already developed more than half of her adult intellectual capacity. After she is eight, no matter what her schooling or environment, her mental abilities can only be altered by about 20%. (*How to Raise a Brighter Child*).

Begin with Your Baby

You can encourage your child's drive to learn from birth by giving her all the freedom you can to explore her environment and her body. When your baby is small, don't leave her alone in a pastel colored crib. Take her around the house with you when she is awake. She can watch the family at work and play from a baby chair, or from a baby carrier strapped to her mother's or father's front or back. You can string toys up in a playpen or across a stroller or crib for her. You can stick colored paper or pictures cut out from magazines on the inside walls of her carrycot

Your little one can learn to pour fluids properly using pots and pans from your kitchen cupboards.

or stroller. When she is ready to crawl, let her do so. Don't imprison her. Remove harmful things from her reach, and give her the freedom to explore. The same applies when she is toddling. There are hundreds of things around your house which she will enjoy examining and playing with. Boxes, kitchen implements, empty jars with screw tops, and so on. At the end of this chapter is a list of books full of ideas about how to help your pre-school child develop her innate drive for competence.

Play Group or Nursery School

Children love to be with others of their own age, and they learn important social lessons from their peers. A play group or nursery school provides for this need, and fortunately, most nursery schools respect children's freedom. They don't force them to sit in chairs and keep quiet and still. If you can find a school in your area which encourages your child to be independent, to respect the property of others, and to pursue her own interests, then by all means, send her there.

The Montessori method

Dr. Maria Montessori lived and worked in the late nineteenth century and the early part of this century. She was struck by the astonishing ability of children to learn in a free environment, and she developed teaching methods which are now to be found in schools all over the world. If you have such a school in your area, you will be doing your child a great service by sending her there. The values she learns will be similar to the ones she is absorbing at home, if you raise her according to the principles outlined in this book. The apparatus in a Montessori school is beautifully maintained, and aimed at appealing specifically to children's different stages of readiness, from two and a half to seven years of age. It is laid out in open cupboards at child level around the room. The children are allowed to work with anything they wish, provided they are ready to use it correctly. The instructress simply shows by example how it should be used. No child may interfere with the work of another, or damage the apparatus. The children are not forced to work, they work because they like to. The activities cover a wide range, including creative work, home activities (like polishing shoes and ironing), reading, writing, math, geography, nature study, and many other subjects. The emphasis is on reality. Montessori believed that the real world is so exciting and challenging for the child that fantasy is superfluous and stems largely from boredom or frustration.

The advantage of a Montessori school over the home is that it provides the opportunity for social development, and offers your child far more varied equipment than you are likely to have at your disposal.

Check on the school first. There are some which call themselves Montessori, but deviate a great deal from the method.

Montessori in the Home

Teaching Montessori in the Home by Elizabeth G. Hainstock tells clearly, with excellent illustrations, exactly how to follow the Montessori teaching methods at home. The advantage of keeping your child at home is that a mother is often the best teacher for her child because she can monitor her development closely and respond when she is ready for a certain new skill.

If She Doesn't Want to Go to School

If your child really does not want to go to play group or nursery school, don't force her to do so. You can try to ease her into it. If she has not been exposed to much other company than your own, she may find the change a little frightening at first. If necessary, stay at school with her for a few days until she is ready to accept your departure.

If she remains frantic at the thought of being left, and hates school, there is no point in sending her. It will only increase her anxiety. She knows what is right for her, and at this stage, she does not have the confidence or security to leave her mother.

A child who is self-sufficient will not have any problems. The first day Leon and I took Justine to our local Montessori school, she was two years and eight months old. I was a little worried about what her reaction would be. I need not have been. She just ran in and started working. When we said goodbye, she looked up as if somewhat put out by the distraction, and said "Goodbye, Mommy and Daddy." So we left, and that was the beginning of a long and happy time for her there. Sometimes she preferred to stay at home. If she chose not to go to school, then she stayed at home. I continued my routine as usual. I did not take time off to entertain her. In two-and-a-half years, she stayed at home about two weeks in all.

Detention without Trial

Mark Twain said, "Don't let your schooling interfere with your education." The real difficulty in preventing this from happening starts when it is time for your child to embark on the State's twelve year schooling sentence. Now, your child must enter upon a long period of probable boredom and frustration. She is going to discover for the first time that learning can be a painful, tedious experience. If she doesn't toe the line, she will be beaten, intimidated, or ridiculed into submission. Her teachers are likely to be thoroughly annoyed if she challenges their authority on the facts they teach or their right to force her to learn what does not interest or concern her. What a tragedy that learning must change from a joy to a penalty.

Your child will probably accumulate some irrelevant, and (to her) uninteresting information which she will forget as fast as she learns it. If she is lucky, she may have teachers in one or two areas who are lively and inspiring. Then she will experience a couple of hours of pleasure a week.

In *What Do I Do Monday?*, John Holt observes: "Indeed the limits we put on facial expression are far more stringent than anything we would find even in a maximum security prison." Not only do the children have to sit still in a desk for most of the day, but often they are expected not to move, speak, or take eyes off the teacher during this time. If they disobey these regulations, they are ridiculed or chastised.

As if that were not enough, they are, in addition, expected to believe that these people who treat them so badly are their friends, and care about their welfare. If they dare to question this self-evident untruth, then they are punished even more severely, and may even be beaten.

Holt goes on to point out: "Most of our schools convey to the child a very powerful message, that they are stupid, worthless, untrustworthy, unfit to make even the smallest decisions about their own lives or learning..." Although school authorities may claim to respect the individuality of our children, and to encourage their growing independence, none of their actions support these assertions.

It is even more damaging, says Holt, to tell children you value and admire them, and then to treat them like fools, than to tell them frankly that you have no respect for them.

A. S. Neill says in *Freedom—Not License!*: "Years ago, in college, I got a grade of 95% in history. If anyone today asked me about some of the simplest facts in British history, I wouldn't be able to answer the questions. Why? Because I was never interested in British History. What good did all that study do me? The time spent in cramming useless facts robbed me of precious hours far better spent doing the things I then liked." (p. 50).

In Neill's school, Summerhill, the children are allowed to learn what interests them. Consequently, says Neill, they often take only a few months to reach the same level of proficiency in a given area which he himself took years to attain. This, he explains, is simply because the children at Summerhill are not bored with their work. How many adults now, asks Neill, can remember anything they learned, for example, in History or Math at school? And how many could care less?

If you want to save your child years of boredom and repression, and possibly severe psychological damage, do all you can to find a school something like Summerhill—a school where she is treated as a free, responsible individual capable of acting in her own self-interest.

All Play and No Work?

Many parents are afraid that if their children are not forced to do so, they will never "work." Apart from hundreds of examples to the contrary in schools like Summerhill and Montessori schools, I would like you to consider this anecdote from *The Continuum Concept* which shows how the work ethic of conventional schooling fails to function.

Jean Liedloff tells the story of Cesar, a Tauripan Indian who had been adopted by Venezuelans and sent to an ordinary school where he learned to read and write, and other conventional "wisdom." As an adult, it came about that he returned to live with his own people. He married a Tauripan girl, had a baby daughter, and settled down on the plantation of a man called Pepe. Here, he was happy to discover that his family could be maintained by Pepe and his sons, who seemed to enjoy doing all the work. Cesar was able to live a life of leisure, doing a little fishing or hunting, which he enjoyed, but otherwise no work at all.

For five years, Cesar lived this way, and then one day he said he would like to start working his own piece of land. Enough time had finally passed to convince him that nobody cared whether he worked or not, and that, if he did so, it would be for his own pleasure. Pepe was very happy to help him clear a piece of land. He said Cesar had been getting bad tempered because he wanted to work, but didn't know it. Pepe found this highly amusing.

My father tells a story of a boy in one of his schools when he was working in education in Kenya. This boy, who was fourteen years old, was a total dud in the classroom. He was completely illiterate, and his teachers had given up hope of drumming anything into his head. His only interest was in electrical things. Since there was no point in keeping him in the classroom, the headmistress decided to let him work on the school's electricity. Very soon after he had started doing this, he miraculously began to read and write. Once the boy had started the electrical work, he discovered that, in order to do it properly, he needed to read. As soon as the motivation was there, he learned to do so easily.

Unfortunately, your children may never get the chance, as Cesar and the African boy did, to find out that they like work. So try never to let them be turned against it in the first place.

Indoctrination

As long as the State owns and controls schools, it will use them for the purpose of indoctrination. The history, religion, and literature that the State deems to be correct will be taught, and the values that the State holds will be presented.

These are the values which maintain that individuals are too stupid and insignificant to decide for themselves what price they should pay for their purchases, whether they should wear seat belts, how long their stores should be open, whether they should observe Sundays, how much they should pay their employees, and so on. The State is "Big Daddy" who will make all the individual's decisions for him, and bale him out if he is in trouble.

These are precisely the opposite values to those which would prevail in a free society, and those which have been put forward in this book.

"...the very essence of a free society is that questions of purpose are to be resolved by the individuals involved. The purposes of education, then, must be personal and individual, to be chosen by the person directly involved, or by those legally responsible for that person." (Benjamin A. Rogge and Pierre F. Goodrich, *Education in a Free Society,* p. 33).

When You Can't Find the Right School

Since schooling is compulsory in most Western countries, if you can't find, or can't afford, a school which allows freedom and encourages independence and self-discipline, you will be forced to send your child to a conventional school.

A. S. Neill tells us that he has hundreds of children writing to him and telling him how they hate school. His answer to them is that he sympathizes, but since they have no choice, they must grin and bear it.

If your children have to go to a conventional school and hate it, you will have to say the same thing to them. Let them know why the run of the mill school is bad. That is the only way to give them a chance to escape the indoctrination and keep their self-esteem intact. Keep the atmosphere at home free, to counterbalance the ill effects, and give them moral support in surviving the system.

When I was in school, I had a particularly authoritarian biology teacher. She used to shut me in the store-room during her class because I "distracted the other girls." When Parents' Day came around, I was a little nervous at the prospect of her meeting my parents, knowing her poor opinion of me. After they had met her, my father said to me, "That old girl's got her soul in a straight-jacket hasn't she?" It was very helpful for me to know that my parents felt the same way I did about her.

If your child is particularly unhappy at a certain school and wishes to attend a different one, then let her do so. Don't force your children to do homework. If they dislike doing it, that is a problem they have to come to terms with in their own way. If they don't do it, it is they who have to suffer the consequences, not you.

If you want to help your children go on learning outside the school system, you will find helpful ideas on how to do so in John Holt's books *What Do I Do Monday?* and *Instead of Education.*

Summary

1. Children have an innate desire to learn.
2. You can help your baby develop her potential by enriching her environment.
3. Montessori schools for preschool children respect their freedom and provide excellent learning opportunities.
4. Most conventional schools have no respect for your children, and may severely damage their natural desire to learn.
5. Try to find a school which adheres to the values of this book. If you cannot, then offer your child moral support to survive the system.

Supplementary Reading

How to Raise a Brighter Child by Joan Beck

Teaching Montessori in the Home by Elizabeth G. Hainstock

What to do when "There's nothing to do" by Boston Children's Medical Centre and Elizabeth M. Gregg

Freedom—Not License! by A. S. Neill

17

Controlling the Mind

In the same way that it is damaging to control your children's actions and decisions, it is also destructive to attempt to control their thoughts and ideas. Parents who try to force their children to believe what they believe and to think what they think usually achieve the opposite. In their striving for independence and individuality, these children rebel in adolescence and develop ideas which they value precisely because they are in conflict with those their parents hold dear.

Censorship

Governments should not censor what people may say, think, read, or view on television or movies. Neither should parents censor their children in this way. Every individual should be able to see, say, and think what he wishes, provided he does not harm anyone else. We all agree that we should be allowed to make our own decisions in these areas.

If we want that freedom for ourselves, then we must grant it to others.

Television

There is a general tendency for people to believe that if children watch violence on TV, they will learn to be violent; however, the primary source of influence on a child's values is his direct experience. If he sees his father regularly hitting his mother, and corporal punishment is the accepted form of discipline in his home, and if, on top of that he watches violence on TV all the time, then certainly he will get the message that violence is OK. His experience will tell him that is the way people generally behave. If he never sees an act of force in his home, if persuasion, discussion, and reason are the order of the day, then he will be able to watch violence on TV or in movies, and read about it in books, and recognize it for the evil that it is.

If you let your child read whatever she likes, she will acquire her own sense of values and widen her horizens.

It is not only the behavior of the parents, but also their attitude which will influence their children. If Mom and Dad sit glued to the television watching violent programs with evident relish, and then tell their child that he must go away because violence is terrible, he will be quick to spot the inconsistency. If parents wish to show their children that they genuinely dislike violence, when something particularly gruesome comes on the screen they can say, "This is horrid, I don't want to watch it. Shall we turn it off and do something else?" Very likely, their child will agree that that is a good idea.

In almost all television programs, it is made pretty clear that the violent man is the "bad guy," and the hero only resorts to violence in self-defense or in order to protect someone else. You can point that out, if you think it is necessary. Most children can see it easily for themselves.

Books

You should allow your child to read whatever books, comics, or other literature he wants. We expose our children to all kinds of disaster in fairy stories without fearing the consequences. We know that if Hansel and Gretel push the witch into an oven, or Jack cuts down the beanstalk causing the giant to come crashing down and sink ten feet into the ground, that our children will not assume that this is the way in which they should deal with people they don't like. By the same token, if they have experienced rationality and pacifism in the home, they will apply those values to the violence they read about in other forms of literature.

You can buy your children the books you approve of, but if they choose to borrow or buy others you don't like, that is their right.

Sexual Violence

In addition to the violence of, for example, robbery, assault, or arson, people often feel that their children should not know about sexual deviation or violence such as rape, sadomasochism, pederasty, homosexuality, and so on. If a child gets hold of pornography, it is usually confiscated forthwith. To do this is really a waste of time. Firstly, the chances are he will read it in secret elsewhere, and secondly, it won't do him any harm. If children see sex between their parents in their own home to be a loving, positive, and healthy experience with no guilt attached to it, they are not going to want to be whipped in order to experience orgasm, or to seduce and rape children when they grow up just because they read that some sick people behave that way.

Unfortunately, violence and sexual deviation are a fact of life. Children will not learn to cope with them or recognize them for what they are and judge them accordingly if they are protected from knowing about them. Sooner or later, they are going to find out the facts of reality, and the younger they are, the clearer their judgment will be because their outlook is more innocent, and they are less riddled with popular misconceptions.

Religion and Philosophy

All parents have opinions on religion, politics, economics, and so on. Even if they have not thought it through very carefully, they have some sort of philosophy of life, some idea of good and bad. Naturally, they would like their children to think and feel the same way they do because they believe that is the right way.

It is important to remember that there are hundreds of different philosophies and religions. Every individual has his own views, which differ to a greater or lesser extent from those of every other individual. You feel quite certain that your beliefs are right, but so is your neighbor sure that his views are right.

You are entitled to try to persuade your child to adopt your values. The best way to do this is to live your philosophy yourself, and let him experience whether it works well for him or not. That may sound obvious, but many people say they believe something, but do not act accordingly. If you want to offer your child your opinions, do so; if he asks for them, certainly do so; but in fairness, point out that this is your view and that other people think differently and should be entitled to.

If you are an atheist, but your child wants to attend a church, or synagogue, or mosque, do not stop him. If you are a staunch Catholic, you have no right to force him to pray twice a day to your God or force him to go to church with you. If you believe that every individual should work for himself and achieve his own ends, and thoroughly disapprove of begging and bumming, that's fine; but if your child wants to subsidize the local children with his hard earned money, or do their homework for them, then that is his choice.

Respect his Views

It is not enough to grant your child the freedom to believe and think as he wishes. Even while granting this freedom, you can damage his self-esteem by belittling or deriding his ideas. Apply the adult test. You don't (or at least shouldn't) say to your friends who come to dinner and offer you their view on life, "Oh, we all go through that stage, you'll grow out of it in time." Or, "Where on earth did you get that crazy idea? I've never heard anything so stupid!" Neither do you greet your friend's opinion on the concept of God with a hoot of laughter.

We all like our children to respect our views. The best way to achieve that is by respecting theirs.

An example of the individuality of children in action took place in the home of some friends of ours. The parents didn't dictate to their children what faith they should hold. The result was that, by the time they reached adolescence, one had adopted the Jewish religion, another had become a Christian, and the third was an atheist!

Summary

1. Your children should have mental as well as physical freedom.

2. Do not censor what your children read or view on TV. Your attitude is the most important influence on them, and they are able to judge good from bad themselves.

3. You may try to persuade your children to accept your values and beliefs, but do not try to force them.

4. Take your children's thoughts and ideas seriously.

18

Adolescence

When children reach adolescence, they experience a great need for total autonomy. This is as it should be, for before long they will have to leave the nest and stand entirely alone.

Adolescents are notorious for their rebelliousness. They are known for their defiance, disobedience, and constant reaction against the advice and admonitions of their parents; however, adolescents who have no authority to rebel against do not behave this way.

When Ginott discusses the teenager, in *Between Parent and Teenager* he observes: "He becomes disobedient and defiant not so much to defy his parents but in order to experience his identity and autonomy."

Everything that has been said in this book up to this point applies at adolescence, and even more so. With younger children, it is often necessary to explain your actions, show how things should be done, and help them to see what the consequences of their actions will be. With your teenagers, all this must fall away, and your children must be treated exactly as you would other adults.

The time has come to accept your children's ability to make decisions for themselves with confidence and trust. If they make mistakes, you must be able to stand back and let them bear the consequences without trying to protect them or betraying fear for them. As Mahatma Gandhi said, "Freedom connotes the right to err."

Chances are, your teenager will be doing a lot of self-examining. She will be wrapped up in learning about herself. She will seem extraordinarily self-centered, and you will be sad to see her experience periods of conflict and depression. The only way you can help is by letting her be. Your task now is to provide a stable, non-judgemental base from which your child can launch herself. All she needs from you is someone she knows she can turn to if she needs to talk; someone she can come to if she wants advice.

Your teenager may be moody and withdrawn at times. Let her be. She is coming to terms with herself and her sexuality.

She still needs the security of a loving and trustful person who tells her by his treatment of her, "I respect you, I have confidence in your ability to do the right thing, I believe you are able to cope with those problems and difficulties which you come up against."

I remember very clearly how my mother illustrated her confidence in me when I was in my early teens. I had a rather wild girl friend named Sue. Her parents had a reputation in the community for being immoral and dissolute. The result was that Sue was not allowed in the homes of several of our contemporaries because their mothers feared her bad influence. When I told my mother this, she said to me, "Sue is welcome in our home. I am not afraid that she will be a bad influence on you; it is far more likely that you will be a good influence on her."

If you rear your children in the manner described in the preceding chapters, your confidence will not be misplaced. They will already have had plenty of experience with independence and will undergo far less conflict and anxiety than most teenagers. They will be in a position to make the move to total autonomy with relative ease.

There are a few specific areas which need to be discussed because they involve particular difficulties for parents.

The Four D's

Driving

Once your children are old enough to obtain a driver's license, you need to decide whether they are going to have access to your car, whether you are going to buy them one of their own, or whether you expect them to work and save for one.

If you decide to buy a car for your child, it is still a good idea to insist that she puts up some of the money. She is far more likely to value and respect something which she has worked toward. Naturally, if the car is hers, you will not dictate how it should be treated, and she will have to maintain it at her own expense. If you decide to let her use your car, it should only be on condition that she looks after it properly. She should drive your car carefully, and pay for repairs if she damages it. She should make sure it has gas and oil when it is returned to you, and should pay for any gas or oil she uses. Naturally, when you need it, it should be returned in the condition in which it was borrowed. If your child does not respect these terms, you should immediately stop lending her your vehicle.

Dating

Your teenagers must decide for themselves how often they go out, and how late they stay up. If they over-extend themselves during the week and it affects their school work, they will discover that for themselves. You can insist that they let you know whether they will be in for meals or not. If they keep missing meals without letting you know, then stop preparing food for them, and let them fend for themselves. You can also request that they give you some idea as to when they expect to be in, so that you do not worry. If your children will not afford you this courtesy, then there is nothing you can do but try to learn not to become anxious. Remember that no news is good news, and you do neither yourself nor your children a favor when you work yourself into a dither if they come in late.

Many parents worry that their daughters will not be safe if they go out with a boy who has a car. They are afraid he might drive dangerously or drink too much. If this is your concern, then say to your daughter, "If you think your friend is a careless driver, or has had too much to drink, feel free to call me any time of the day or night, and I will fetch you or give you a lift." Another alternative, used successfully by friends who have three teenage daughters, is to open an account with a local taxi company. Whenever one of their girls wants to leave a party where drugs appear, or would rather not risk driving home with drunken friends, she calls a cab. The parents settle the account at the end of the month, and consider it money well spent. They find their girls prefer this arrangement to calling them, and use it sensibly. You cannot do more than that.

Sexual freedom for adolescents has been dealt with in the chapter on sex.

Drinking

Your children will develop their attitude toward alcohol from your drinking habits in the home. If you do have a drink occasionally, then it is a good idea to offer them a glass of wine or beer when you have one. That way they will learn to handle alcohol naturally and sensibly. Provided they have a free environment and have learned self-discipline, they will not turn to drink as an act of rebellion.

When I was seventeen and had just completed high school, I went to a party where some boys mixed me a couple of lethally strong drinks. I had no idea what was in them. I became dis astrously drunk, and horribly sick. The next day, I went to my parents' room and, bursting into tears, told my father, who was lying in bed, that I had been drunk. I expected a strongly-worded lecture. Instead, he smiled and gave me a hug saying, "That happens to most people at least once. Now you will know why you should be careful in the future." His sympathetic and non-judgmental attitude saved me a lot of guilt, and reaffirmed my belief that I was sensible enough to learn from my mistakes.

Drugs

Teenagers who get involved in taking drugs do so for a number of reasons. Among these are rebelliousness, a desire to go along with the crowd, and an attempt to escape reality. A child from a secure and free home will not need to rebel. She will have a strong sense of self-worth, and therefore will not rely on the approval of her peers for her self-esteem, and she will not need to escape a reality in which she feels happy and in control. In a home where all subjects are discussed freely, the topic of drugs is sure to arise, so she will not be ignorant about their ill-effects. She will also have learned from the media how dangerous they all are (apart from marijuana). The point to make about marijuana is that, though many studies indicate that it is no more harmful than alcohol or cigarettes, it is illegal. The penalties attached to breaking the law make it not worth while taking the chance.

If your child is already a heavy drinker or drug addict, this is not the time for lectures or recriminations. It is time to get help fast, for both yourself and your child. *Between Parent and Teenager* (Haim Ginott) and *Bringing up Children in a Difficult Time* (Dr. B. Spock) both deal well with how to go about finding help.

Property Rights Disputes

Of course you will expect your teenagers to respect the property of the other members of the family, just as you respect theirs. If they are careless or thoughtless, remember that they are going through a stage of tremendous self-discovery. Often their carelessness is due to self-absorption and is quite unintentional, and you only need draw attention to it for it to be remedied.

In every family, problems will arise in areas related to property rights, such as who should have their favorite television channel on, or how loudly stereos should be played, or how long one person may occupy the bathroom. Certainly, by adolescence, and preferably even before, it is a good idea to have a family get-together every so often to discuss the grievances of the different members of the family and decide how they can be resolved. These meetings should not be taken as an opportunity for parents to lay down the law, but as a time for children to learn to compromise and find ways in which all the members of the family can live happily together.

The family might decide, for example, that Gerry can play his record player as loudly as he likes, provided he first sound-proofs his room with egg-boxes. They might decide to establish a rotating schedule for first choice of television channel, or work out a timetable for the use of the bathroom.

Allow your children to develop at their own rate. Pushing them into growing up, dating, wearing makeup, or whatever you think is the correct behavior for an adolescent, is as bad as forbidding them to do certain things. When it comes to clothes and makeup, again let them decide and choose for themselves. You can rely on peer group ressure to prevent them from doing anything too outrageous, and if it doesn't, it is still not your job to interfere.

Your reward for respecting your teenager's freedom will be that, when the time comes for her to leave home, she will do so, not as a hateful and unhappy enemy, but as your friend and confidante.

Summary

1. Your teenagers should be allowed total autonomy. They should be treated exactly as you would other adults.

2. When problems arise, you should get together with your teenagers to discuss them and discover solutions.

Supplementary Reading

Bringing up Children in a Difficult time by Dr. B. Spock

Between Parent and Teenager by Dr. Haim G. Ginott.

19

Untying the Knot

When you read this book, your children may be any age between new-born and twenty. You may think these ideas make a lot of sense, but at the same time feel that you have been doing things so differently up to now that making the change will be an impossible task. Tying a knot is so much easier than untying one.

The younger your child is, the easier it will be to implement the methods in the preceding chapters. Up to the age of about three, you can simply set about systematically changing the way you have been relating to them. You can give him easy explanations of your behavior that he will understand. Say, for example, that you have a two-year-old who throws tantrums every time he wants something. He does this because he has learned that, as soon as he opens his mouth and yells, Mommy and Daddy rush to give him whatever he wants so that he will close it again. Now, you want him to learn that people will only do things for him when he asks politely. The lesson is going to be a difficult one for both of you. He will be bewildered because, suddenly, his actions are not causing the expected result and, to begin with, he will probably throw twice as many tantrums as before. You are going to have to hold fast to your resolve, and be firm and consistent.

If applying these methods is sometimes painful, remember that the sooner they are applied, the less pain there will be, and the quicker everyone will benefit. This is the principle of short-term pain for long-term pleasure.

When your two-year-old starts to scream, you must say firmly, "Nobody is going to help you when you make that noise. If you want something, you must ask nicely." In the beginning, this is likely to have no effect at all, except that he will double up on the volume. Then, you must decide whether you can stand to stay in the room and ignore the tantrum, or whether you should leave or move him out of earshot until the storm has passed. Respond promptly to any requests he does make politely. This does not mean you must give him anything and everything he asks for, provided his tone of voice is pleasant, but that you should accede immediately when his requests are reasonable, so that his acceptable behavior is positively reinforced. If he asks pleasantly for something you choose not to give him, explain why. Provided you are completely consistent, it will only take a few days, or at most weeks, before the tantrums cease.

From the age of four years on, it is a good idea to discuss in more detail with your child the changes you intend making. You can say, for instance, "I have been doing some thinking, and I have decided I am not always fair to you, and I do not always insist that you be fair with me. From now on, you are not allowed to damage my things, but I will let you do whatever you like with yours," or "From now on I am going to pay you for work you do for me, just as Daddy is paid for work he does in the office," or whatever other change you have decided to bring about. If your child is old enough, give him this book to read, and ask him what he thinks about it. Discuss how you can go about putting the ideas into practice.

In the beginning, you will need a lot of patience and self-discipline when you make changes. You will find yourself slipping back into old patterns, and you will have to monitor yourself continually, until the new ways become habits. Your child will be confused by your changed reactions and behavior, and you may need to explain several times why you are now doing things differently.

Many readers will find that they have, possibly without too

much thought, already been doing many of the things I suggest. For them, a few new changes will be easy to implement; but for those who feel they must embark on a radically new program, possibly with an older child, the most important thing of all to aim for is absolute consistency. Children are very sensitive to inconsistency, and will lose trust quickly if they sense it. If you do fall back into old ways, the best thing to do is to point out your mistakes and apologize.

Over the years, your child may have become very dependent on your making all his decisions for him. It will not be easy for either of you, when you begin to withdraw support. Take it slowly; let him first practice making small decisions, such as what he should eat or wear, before he starts making major ones.

If you have teenagers, remember that soon they must leave home and be self-supporting, and the more practice they get while you are still around to provide fundamental security, and hopefully a sounding board too, the more likely they are to cope later. Let them jump in the deep end of independence now, and prove to you and themselves that they can swim.

Because consistency is so important, you should make every effort to persuade your partner to read this book, too. If that is not possible, at least present the ideas to him for discussion. If only one parent respects his child's property and freedom, and demands the same in return, that will be better than nothing; however, your children's response will be quicker and more gratifying if both partners apply the same values.

If your partner is an authoritarian person who insists on continuing to lay down the law, and refuses to respect his children's rights, then you will have to explain to your children that, although you believe their other parent's attitude is wrong, they will have to abide by his rules as long as they live in this house.

You may examine your relationship with your child and feel that you have made so many mistakes that now it is really too late to undo the damage; however, there is considerable evidence that this is never the case.

In *Mothering*, Rudolph Schaeffer says that the effects of experience on a child's personality are far from being irreversible: "The notion that parents can exert a particularly profound influence during the first few years—an influence that will remain throughout life and cannot be eradicated by subsequent experience—is certainly widespread.... Yet faith, rather than fact, is what such a belief is built on. Human development is rather more complicated, rather less rigidly determined than such a view suggests." What evidence we have, although it is not conclusive, suggests that a single experience—no matter how traumatic it may be, or how early it occurs in the individual's life, seldom if ever causes an ineradicable impression. Schaeffer points out that this is just as well. If we were to accept that a child's personality could not be altered or affected after the first few years, we would not bother to try and help children who had been harmed during this time: nor would we consider subsequent experience to be of any value to older children.

Schaeffer goes on to discuss various studies which indicate that, although the individual is more sensitive to particular types of influence at some developmental stages than others, there seems to be no one specific critical period in which his whole character is formed. Even severe "retardation in the first year or two of life is reversible, and early experiences, however drastic at the time, do not necessarily set up patterns of behavior that cannot subsequently be modified."

What this tells us is that, no matter how antisocial your child seems to be, if you begin now to treat him as a person worthy of respect and consideration, he will change for the better.

Summary

1. If you have been doing things wrong and want to change to the methods in this book:
   (a.) be completely consistent, and
   (b.) remember the short-term pain you both experience is in the interest of long-term pleasure.

2. If you have older children, ask them to read this book, and discuss it with them.

3. Don't despair! If you treat your child with respect, eventually he will respond.

20

The Ultimate Child

The following list of ten basic rules sums up all that has been said in the preceding chapters:

1. Provided he does not harm other people or their property, every person should be free to act as he chooses.

2. Children are rational and logical, and want to be happy, just as we do.

3. The only important difference between adults and children is experience.

4. Whenever you are not sure how you should respond to your child's actions, apply the Adult Test. Ask yourself, "What would I do if this were an adult?"

5. Children learn best by example and experience; therefore, if we want them to respect us, then we must respect them.

6. The three main qualities you need to foster in your child's personality are independence, self-esteem, and individuality.

7. Children do not have an innate need to be contrary. They want to conform to the standards of those around them.

8. When your child behaves badly, the first place to look for the cause is in your own actions. You are the most important influence in your child's life, and therefore you are most likely to be the cause of her bad behavior.

9. Every time a human being acts volitionally, he exchanges a situation he has for one he prefers.

10. If applying these methods is sometimes painful, remember that the sooner they are applied, the less pain there will be, and the sooner everyone will benefit. This is the principle of short-term pain for long-term pleasure.

If you make these ten rules the basis of your relationship with your children, you can expect them to develop the following characteristics:

They will be individualistic, assertive, and self-confident. They will not go along like sheep with the opinions of the crowd, but judge the rightness or wrongness of their own or other people's actions according to a clearly defined set of values.

They will have true self-esteem. They will not depend on the approval of others for their happiness. They will like themselves, and consequently find it easy to make good and true friends.

They will respect the freedom of others to believe what they wish, and to do as they choose with their lives. They will be indignant if they are not granted the same freedom. They will not reject the opinions of others dogmatically, but consider them with reason. They will always be open to new ideas and viewpoints, and ready to learn new things. They will feel no need to prove to others that they are right, or force others to accept their values.

They will have much to teach you. They will enjoy work as something positive and productive. They will not want sympathy or charity, but will expect to have their work acknowledged and paid for at its market value.

They will want to relate to people they regard as their equals, and to be loved and admired, not in spite of their weaknesses, but because of their strengths. They will not wish to be supported emotionally or physically, nor will they need to be needed by others. They will have little sympathy for parasites and spongers.

They will be responsible and decisive, and learn from their errors, rather than being destroyed by them.

They will be open and honest, and communicate easily with others. They will make compromises which accommodate the needs of those close to them without making sacrifices.

They will not turn to drugs such as alcohol or nicotine to make life more manageable. They will not be aggressive or violent.

They will treat their bodies with respect, eating healthily and exercising regularly. They will enjoy sex uninhibitedly without feelings of guilt, and without perversion.

Above all, they will be happy and positive, and look upon life as a challenge they enjoy meeting.

Bibliography

Adams, Paul, Leila Berg, Nan Berger, Michael Duane, A. S. Neil and Robert Ollendorff. *Children's Rights.* New York: Praeger, 1971.

Babcock, Dorothy E. and Terry D. Keepers. *Raising Kids O.K.* New York: Avon Books, 1976.

Bartz, Wayne R., Ph.D. and Richard A. Rasor, Ed.D. *Surviving with Kids.* New York: Ballantine Books, 1980.

Beck, Joan. *How to Raise a Brighter Child.* London: Fontana, 1978.

Boston Children's Medical Center and Elizabeth M. Gregg. *What to do When "There's Nothing to do".* London: Arrow, 1971.

Bowlby, John. *Separation: Anxiety and Anger.* Vol. 11 of *Attachment and Loss,* Harmondsworth: Penguin, 1975.

Barleigh, Ann Husted, ed. *Education in a Free Society.* Indianapolis, IN: Liberty Fund, 1973.

Clark, Le Mon, M.D. *The Enjoyment of Love in Marriage.* New York: Signet, 1969.

Comfort, Alex and Jane. *The Facts of Love.* London: Mitchell Beazley, 1979.

Conran, Shirley. *Superwoman.* Harmondsworth: Penguin, 1977.

Corkill Briggs, Dorothy. *Your Child's Self-Esteem.* New York: Doubleday, 1975.

Davis, Adelle. *Let's Have Healthy Children.* New York: Signet, 1972.

Faber, Adele and Elaine Mazlish. *Liberated Parents Liberated Children.* New York: Avon Books, 1975.

Fass, Jerome S., M.D. *How to Raise an Emotionally Healthy Child.* New York: Pocket Books, 1969.

Gesell, Arnold. *The First Five Years of Life*. London: Methuen, 1950.

Gesell, Arnold, Frances L. Ilg, and Louise Bates Ames. *The Child from Five to Ten*. London: Hamish Hamilton, 1965.

Gibran, Kahlil. *The Prophet*. London: William Heinemann, 1971.

Ginott, Dr. Haim G. *Between Parent and Child*. London: Pan Books, 1976.

Ginott, Dr. Haim G. *Between Parent and Teenager*. New York: Avon, 1973.

Goodman, Paul. *Compulsory Miseducation*. Harmondsworth: Penguin, 1973.

Hainstock, Elizabeth G. *Teaching Montessori in the Home*. New York: Random House, 1968.

Holt, John. *Instead of Education*. Harmondsworth: Penguin, 1977.

Holt, John. *What Do I Do Monday?* New York: Delta, 1970.

Hymes, James L., Jr. *The Child Under Six*. Englewood: Prentice Hall, 1963.

Jolly, Hugh. *Book of Child Care*. London: Sphere Books, 1977.

Kitzinger, Sheila. *Women as Mothers*. Glasgow: Fontana, 1978.

La Léche League Manual. *The Womanly Art of Breast Feeding*. London: Tandem, 1976.

Leach, Penelope. *Babyhood*. Harmondsworth: Penguin Books, 1976.

Liedloff, Jean. *The Continuum Concept*. London: Futura, 1976.

Lillard, Paula Polk. *Montessori: A Modern Approach*. New York: Schocken, 1978.

Malinowski, Branislaw. *Sex and Repression in Savage Society*. London: Routledge, 1961.

Minshull, Ruth. *Miracles for Breakfast*. Ann Arbor, MI 1972.

Montagu, Ashley. *Touching*. London: Harper and Row, 1979.

Montessori, Maria. *The Child in the Family*. London: Pan, 1975.

Montessori, Maria. *The Discovery of the Child*. New York: Ballantine, 1976.

Neill, A. S. *Freedom—Not License!* New York: Hart, 1966.

Nicolson, John. *Habits.* London: Pan 1977.

Postman, Neil and Charles Weingartner. *Teaching as Subversive Activity.* Harmondsworth: Penguin, 1973.

Prescott, James W. "Body Pleasure and the Origins of Violence" in *The Futurist,* April 1975. Washington DC World Future Soc.

Pulaski, Mary Ann Spencer, Ph.D. *Your Baby's Mind and How it Grows.* New York: Harper and Row, 1978.

Schaffer, Rudolph. *Mothering.* London: Fontana, 1977.

Scharlatt, Elizabeth L., ed. *Kids: Day In and Day Out.* New York: Simon and Schuster, 1979.

Spock, Dr. Benjamin. *Baby and Child Care.* 3rd ed., London: Bodley Head, 1973.

Spock, Dr. Benjamin. *Bringing Up Children in Difficult Times.* London: Nel, 1977.

Storr, Anthony. *Sexual Deviation.* London: Heinemann, 1965.

Thevenin, Tine. *The Family Bed.* Minneapolis: Tine Thevenin, 1976.

Valentine, C. W. *The Normal Child (and Some of His Abnormalities).* Harmondsworth: Penguin, 1972.

Wolfgang, Michael S. *Male and Female Sexual Deviations.* Los Angeles: Sherbourne Press, 1964.

Yates, Alayne. *Sex Without Shame.* London: Futura, 1980.

Index